Charles Truman Wyckoff

Feudal relations between the kings of England and Scotland

Under the early Plantagenets

Charles Truman Wyckoff

Feudal relations between the kings of England and Scotland
Under the early Plantagenets

ISBN/EAN: 9783743347489

Manufactured in Europe, USA, Canada, Australia, Japa

Cover: Foto ©ninafisch / pixelio.de

Manufactured and distributed by brebook publishing software (www.brebook.com)

Charles Truman Wyckoff

Feudal relations between the kings of England and Scotland

The University of Chicago
FOUNDED BY JOHN D. ROCKEFELLER

FEUDAL RELATIONS

BETWEEN THE

KINGS OF ENGLAND AND SCOTLAND

UNDER THE EARLY PLANTAGENETS

A DISSERTATION SUBMITTED TO THE FACULTIES OF THE GRADUATE
SCHOOLS OF ARTS, LITERATURE, AND SCIENCE, IN CANDIDACY
FOR THE DEGREE OF DOCTOR OF PHILOSOPHY

DEPARTMENT OF HISTORY

BY
CHARLES TRUMAN WYCKOFF

CHICAGO
The University of Chicago Press
1897

The University of Chicago
FOUNDED BY JOHN D. ROCKEFELLER

FEUDAL RELATIONS

BETWEEN THE

KINGS OF ENGLAND AND SCOTLAND

UNDER THE EARLY PLANTAGENETS

A DISSERTATION SUBMITTED TO THE FACULTIES OF THE GRADUATE
SCHOOLS OF ARTS, LITERATURE, AND SCIENCE, IN CANDIDACY
FOR THE DEGREE OF DOCTOR OF PHILOSOPHY

DEPARTMENT OF HISTORY

BY
CHARLES TRUMAN WYCKOFF

CHICAGO
The University of Chicago Press
1897

TABLE OF CONTENTS.

		Page
INTRODUCTION		v
CHAPTER I.	The "Great Commendation"	1
CHAPTER II.	The Cessions of Cumberland and Lothian	19
CHAPTER III.	Norman Influence in Scotland	33
CHAPTER IV.	The Reign of the First Plantagenet	64
CHAPTER V.	Treaty of Falaise and Charter of Release	77
CHAPTER VI.	The Period of the Great Charter	95
CHAPTER VII.	The Reign of Alexander II	115
CHAPTER VIII.	The Reign of Alexander III	129
BIBLIOGRAPHY		155

INTRODUCTION.

The exact nature and extent of the feudal relations existing between the crowns of England and Scotland have been a fiercely mooted question. It lost its practical interest for the people at large with the permanent union of the two kingdoms in May, 1707. This union, on terms of complete independence and perfect equality, marks the abandonment of the early English claims, and indicates the just basis on which the Scotch claims are grounded.[1]

Nature of Subject

In May, 1604, Lord Bacon prepared a draft of "An Act for the better grounding of a further Union to ensue between the Kingdoms of England and Scotland." In his report of a conference with the lords he gives "the reasons of the lower house *in point of law*, in the question whether the Scots born since the King [James] came to the crown be naturalized in England."

Both of these passages have a bearing on the present discussion.

The first speaks of

.... these two ancient and mighty kingdoms, which have been *so many ages united in continent and language*, but *separated* in sovereignty and allegiance ....

The second gives the reasons of the Commons against naturalization :

There is no subordination of the crown of Scotland to the crown of England, but they stand as distinct and entire souverainties ; whereas Aquitaine, Anjou, and other places in France were subordinate to this crown, as appears by good records that a *corpus capias* or any writ under the great seal was of force among them, and they had access here for there complaints in Parliament.[2]

[1] For the Act of Union see *Journal of the House of Commons*, XV, 1705-1707.
[2] Works, III, pp. 204, 329-30.

v

But though the union removed the question from the sphere of practical politics, it did not lose its scholastic interest. How intense that interest had been was apparent when Rymer, who began the "Foedera" in 1693, discovered and published what purported to be a charter[1] of homage by Malcolm Ceanmore and his son to Edward the Confessor. It proved to be a gross forgery from the pen of John Hardyng, the poet and chronicler, who had deposited it in the treasury in 1457. He professed to have obtained it and other documents, in Scotland, at great expense and at the hazard of his life. James I (of Scotland), he said, had offered him 1,000 marks in gold to give them up. King Henry VI rewarded him with a life pension of £20 *per annum*. The publication of this charter just at a time when union was being discussed created great excitement. Writers took up the cudgels on both sides. The arguments of William Atwood "had the distinction of being burned by the Edinburgh hangman, at the command of the Scottish Parliament."[2]

Recent Writers

Among recent writers on this subject two deserve especial mention, though their notes and appendices relating to it form only a small part of works on other topics. The author of "The History of Scotland under Her Early Kings" handles in a masterly way a period dismissed by other historians as dark, fabulous, and unworthy their attention.[3] The results of his work, so far as it relates to purely Scottish history, have been generally accepted as scholarly and authoritative. Mr. Robertson incidentally introduces much valuable material in proof of the independence of the kingdom of Scotland, though such proof is not the real purpose of his work.

This position Mr. Freeman, in his "Norman Conquest," systematically combats, insisting that from A. D. 924–1328 the

---

[1] Palgrave, Docts. and Records, I, p. cxcvii ; Bain, Cal. Docts., I, pp. xii and 1.

[2] Bain, Cal. Docts., I, p. xi.

[3] E. W. Robertson. I am greatly indebted to his invaluable guidance. *Cf.* also Skene, Celtic Scotland, and Burton, History of Scotland.

entire kingdom of Scotland was in a state of *legal and permanent dependence* on the English "Emperor;" that during this time "the vassalage of Scotland was an essential part of the public law of the isle of Britain."[1] In his essay on "The Relations between the Crowns of England and Scotland" he complains because so many of his countrymen condemn Edward's assertion of rights as unjust and illegal, and sympathize with the Scots in the struggle to maintain their independence in the face of overwhelming numbers.[2] This feeling on the part of Englishmen themselves is one more of the slender twigs of testimony which, though weak singly, together form an unbreakable bundle of proof in favor of the justice and truth of the claims of Scotland.

It was an often expressed desire of Mr. Freeman's to take up this topic and discuss it at length. "The subject," he says, "is one excellently suited for a monograph."[3] But death came before the desire could be realized. Mr. Robertson's death had occurred a short time before the criticisms on his work were made. Nothing of note has been written since on either side, beyond brief references to the works of these two men. Since so eminent and recent a writer as Mr. Freeman has attempted to maintain in the most absolute terms the dependence of the *kingdom* of Scotland on her imperial overlord, it cannot be deemed a work of supererogation to review the subject in the light of all the materials now accessible. The interests of all who seek to know what is authentic history demand such a reconsideration of traditional theories.

In taking up the subject afresh, a brief glance at the origin and early history of the people who inhabited North Britain will be necessary. It will also be imperative to keep several points constantly in mind:

Important Considerations

1. The sources are largely from English writers, who may naturally be expected to show a bias in favor of their own land and

---

[1] Norman Conquest, I, p. 59.
[2] Hist. Essays, First Series, 4th ed.
[3] Norman Conq., I, Note G.

king—especially when, as in the case of monastic chroniclers, that king was the source of their bounty. The paucity of historical material in Scotland is due to several causes. One writer charges it to the "malicious policy" of Edward I of England, who, in order to establish his claim to feudal supremacy over Scotland,

Sources Largely English; Possibly Biased. Reasons

.... seized the public archives, ransacked churches and monasteries, and getting possession by force or fraud, of many historical monuments, which tended to prove the antiquity or freedom of the kingdom [Scotland], carried some of them into England, and commanded the rest to be burnt.

This opinion is based on a statement in Innes' "Essay."[1] In his preface, however, Innes somewhat qualifies the position taken in the main body of his work. Edward, by a writ dated August 12, 1291, at Berwick-on-Tweed, required

.... all the charters instruments rolls and writs whatsoever that might concern the rights of the competitors, or his own pretended title to the superiority of Scotland, to be carried off and placed where he should appoint; and these to be put into the hands of five persons, two Scots and three English; and these last to act by themselves, if the two first happened to be hindered. All which was accordingly executed, and all either lost or destroyed, or carried up to London; whereof the remains of our records, partly printed by M. Rymer, partly to be met with as yet in the Tower of London and archives of Westminster, make too evident a proof.[2]

Another writ, published by Rymer, certifies that on the coronation of King John, in 1292, certain documents were delivered on his behalf to Alexander de Balliol, chamberlain of Scotland, at Roxburgh Castle. The catalogue, which gives only a general statement of the number and contents of the various "sacks, hanapers and pyxes, ... is too vague to warrant more than a mere guess" as to what documents were included.[3] Innes well says:

[1] W. Robertson, Hist. Scot.; Innes' Essay, p. 303; Memoir, p. xxv.
[2] Innes' Essay, p. 305.   [3] Bain, I, p. vii.

I have some doubt whether King Edward, having during the confusions of a divided and headless nation, gotten himself declared superior lord of Scotland, would be so very scrupulous as to restore back those very special records by which that superiority had been renounced by his predecessors, and Scotland acknowledged as an independent kingdom, such as the charter of release granted by King Richard I to King William, since it still remains in England, and was very candidly published by M. Rymer, from the original.[1]

A document generally called by historians "An inventory taken of the Scotch Records at the time of their being brought into the Exchequer at London by King Edward the First" found its way to the English Exchequer. It is said to be in reality "a schedule of all the bulls, charters, and other muniments in the King of Scotland's Treasury at Edinburgh on Michaelmas day 1282 (three years before the death of Alexander III). . . . Whatever became of these," says Mr. Bain, "it is pretty certain that nothing but the mere inventory ever reached the English Exchequer." It hardly seems possible, however, that such a collection of documents could have escaped the rigorous search instituted by Edward. The presence of the inventory in the English Exchequer ought also to be good presumptive evidence, all other proof being wanting, that the articles recorded in it accompanied it. It is said Edward's anxiety "was rather to discover than to suppress writings, as is clear from his many writs to the religious houses of his kingdom, commanding search to be made for evidence in support of his claims of superiority." It is true he ransacked the records far and wide to get support for his claims, but it may be fairly questioned what would have been the fate—in the hot partisanship of that period, and among the adherents of the powerful king—of a document which clearly proved that he had no claim to a feudal overlordship in Scotland.[2]

But these long-suffering records were to endure worse things at the hands of fate. King John had hardly won in his appeal before he renounced his homage and allegiance to the English

[1] Innes, as above.   [2] Bain, I, p. vii.

crown, "wearied with King Edward's provocations, with the reproaches of his subjects, and probably of his own conscience.' A league with Philip of France called down the vengeance of Edward, who,

.... intending to ruin entirely the monarchy, and abolish the regal dignity among the Scots, the better to secure his title of superior lord over them, carried off not only the public records, but the regalia, and even the famous stone chair on which our kings used to be crowned.

There is little doubt that Edward intended, if possible, to reduce Scotland to the same condition as Wales. Under the brave Bruce the tide was turned, and at York, in 1328, in a writ sanctioned by Parliament and sealed with the great seal, Edward III was compelled to solemnly renounce "all title, right, and pretension to any superiority over the kingdom of Scotland; and to declare null and of no force all past acts, writs, and conventions to the contrary."[1]

Another factor in the destruction of the Scottish records was John Knox and the Scottish reformers, who faithfully carried out their maxim, "The surest means to hinder the rooks to come back was to burn their nests." Cromwell also had a part in their destruction.[2]

About the close of the fourteenth century John of Fordun made an effort to gather up the then existing fragments of Scottish history, and compiled a chronicle "in a new form, that suited best with the taste of the times in which he wrote." He sought for material in England and Ireland, as well as in Scotland, talking with learned men and jotting down all the bits of information he could find. A chronicle based on such fragments and on the hearsay of centuries naturally has little weight. For the later period his work becomes more valuable, but his continuators and revisers are not trustworthy. His imitators, Boece,

---

[1] Innes' Essay, pp. 11-12. There was an old prophecy that wherever the famous Stone of Destiny was, there Scottish kings should rule. It was placed under the coronation chair in Westminster Abbey, and the prophecy seemed fulfilled when James VI of Scotland became James I of England. (Gardiner, Students' Hist. of Eng., p. 219.)

[2] Bain, I, p. ix.

whose work is "stuffed with fables," and Buchanan, who followed Boece simply because it favored his designs against monarchy, are still less reliable.

But not only must our sources and authorities be sought among English writers; they are also

Sources for Pre-Feudal Period Receive Feudal Coloring
2. From men who almost without exception lived and wrote after the Norman Conquest had brought in feudal ideas, institutions, and language. Where they draw their materials from earlier writers, the narrative usually receives a feudal coloring under their hands, if it does not become absolutely corrupt. Stubbs, referring to certain parts of Walter of Coventry, says:

I dare not say that this part of the work is of any historical value. It illustrates the way in which history was used politically, during the struggle with Scotland, and it has afforded us some slight hints as to the circumstances under which the compilation was made.[1]

Mr. Robertson says:

The claims grounded in the feudal era on the *chronicled* dependence of the Scots upon the Anglo-Saxon Monarchy before the Conquest, may be said to rest either upon passages interpolated in a true text; actual forgeries and fabrications; or else upon amplifications and exaggerations of the truth.

An example of the first class is the story (in Simeon of Durham) of Malcolm's meeting with King Edward in 1059. The editor of the Rolls Series notes that this is a *marginal* entry of a later date than the text. Mr. Robertson continues:

As Roger Hoveden, who at the opening of the 13th Century, copied the whole of Simeon's chronicle word for word in his own, has omitted all notice of it, the entry,—of which the object is unmistakable, —must have been added to the original ms. at a very late date, and, once incorporated with the body of the work, has been falsely stamped with the almost contemporary authority of Simeon.[2]

The ancient laws of William the Conqueror also afford an interesting illustration of the way in which an historical basis for

[1] Walt. Cov., I, p. xxxiv.
[2] Sim. Dun., II, p. 174; Hoveden, An. 1059; Early Kings, II, pp. 385–6.

the claim of feudal supremacy arose. The author of the "Select Charters" says:

> The following short record, which is found in this, its earliest form, in the 'Textus Rofensis,' a ms. written during the reign of Henry I, contains what is probably the sum and substance of all the legal enactments actually made by the Conqueror, independent of his confirmation of earlier laws; they are probably the alterations or emendations referred to by Henry I in his charter, as made by his father in the laws of King Edward.

It reads thus:

> In primis quod .... pacem et securitatem inter Anglos et Normannos servari. Statuimus etiam ut omnis liber homo foedere et sacramento affirmet, quod infra et extra Angliam Willelmo regi fideles esse volunt.

Compare with this the record as it was moulded to suit the purposes of later writers:

> Statuimus .... pacem, et securitatem, et concordiam, judicium, et justiciam inter Anglos et Normannos, Francos et Britones, Walliae et Cornubiae, Pictos et Scotos Albanie, similiter inter Francos et insulanos ....
>
> Statuimus .... intra et extra universum regnum Anglie (quod olim vocabatur regnum Britannie) ....[1]

It must be noted,

3. That the physical features of Britain favor the *theory* of an English overlordship, but are against the *practical realization* of such a claim. In fertility, in acreage, in population, England has a great advantage. One writer on the subject estimates the relative populations as one to six or seven. This was taken into account in adjusting the relative amount of taxes at the time of the union. To offset

Influence of Physical Conditions

---

[1] Stubbs, Sel. Charters, pp. 83-4; Thorpe, Anc. Laws, I, p. 490; Hoveden (An. 1180) gives these laws in their simpler form. *Cf.* also the statement that Edgar was rowed on the Dee by six or eight kings, among them the King of Scots. Robertson shows this is a fabrication. Even Freeman admits that "William of Malmesbury or even Florence of Worcester may have blundered or exaggerated about Edgar's triumph at Chester." (Early Kings, II, p. 386; Norman Conq., I, Notes G and Q; Burton, Hist. Scot., I, p. 331.)

this, however, is the fact that nature has marked out Scotland as the home of independence—"a country well adapted for union and defence."[1] Two mountain ranges, intersecting at right angles, form the backbone of the land, and furnish a safe base for attack, sudden retreat, and the overwhelming defeat of an enemy who dares penetrate these defenses of nature. A rugged climate, and a soil from which the fruits of nature can be obtained only through diligence, favor the development of a hardy, warlike race, while the fertile south tempts them to pillage, and thus to the acquirement of skill in war. They imitated the example of the Teuton rather than of the Celt, in that they avoided walled cities, as traps, and fought in the open, where they could make a sudden onset against their foes, or an equally sudden retreat, if necessary, to the fastnesses of their native hills. Such warfare is preëminently difficult to meet and overcome, as in the case of the Germanic tribes in conflict with Rome, the Saxon opposition to the might of Charles the Great, the successful struggle of the Swiss cantons for independence, and eventually of Scotland herself.

4. The conscientious student can hardly hope to see this subject in its true light, unless he views the history of Scotland

Must View History in its Entirety as a whole, and not in detached periods. He will then be impressed with the fact that this history shows certain continuous characteristics. It begins with a warlike, independent people, who constantly resist any encroachment on their rights and liberties. Weak or handicapped kings may be untrue and bring their appeals to the English king, in the hope of gaining thereby what they could otherwise never have. But they soon pass away, while the struggle goes on. At length, the great object which has been the cause of struggle for centuries—an object at first dimly perceived, or only felt instinctively, but constantly growing in clearness and force with the growth of a national consciousness—is attained, and Scotland comes into the full possession of her birth-right. This is the true inference to draw from these centuries of dis-

[1] Burns, Scot. War of Indep., I, p. 16 (1874); Burton, Hist. Scot., I, p. 83.

pute. They witnessed claims put forth only to be strenuously denied, and in the end successfully resisted.[1]

It is necessary to turn now for a moment to the beginnings of Scottish history. In the early Christian era the north of Britain was inhabited by a number of savage, warlike tribes, who were at once a menace to the Roman power, and the terror of the native Britons. The Scots proper came from Ireland at an early date — certainly by A. D. 502 — and settled in the region north of the Firth of Clyde. Farther north and east were other tribes, the Picts predominating. South of the Clyde the Britons found a temporary refuge in the regions known later as Strathclyde and Cumbria, while east of them lay a group of Saxons or Angles. These early centuries are full of warfare and shifting populations, and call up many complicated and still disputed questions. But the accession of Kenneth MacAlpin, in 843 A. D.,[2] furnishes a safe starting point for historical investigation. It is no longer considered probable that the true Scots, to which line Kenneth belonged, could have conquered or exterminated the larger body of Picts.[3] But whether by a gradual process of amalgamation, or otherwise, in the twelfth year of his reign over the Scots he was recognized as king of the Picts also, the united kingdom being bounded on the south by the Clyde and the Forth. The supremacy of the Scots was due in part to their superior civilization. Their literature was supreme before the spread of Anglo-Saxon literature had begun. Their scholars were welcomed everywhere. They stigmatized the Saxons as barbarians, just as a Roman might have done. Even the patriotic Beda concedes the civilizing influence which came to the Saxons from Iona.[4]

Early History

Kenneth MacAlpin, 843 A. D.

---

[1] Burton, Hist. Scot., II, p. 1.

[2] 844 A. D., Skene, Celtic Scot., I, p. 309.

[3] Kenneth's Scottish kingdom included only the modern shires of Perth, Fife, Stirling, Dumbarton, and the larger part of the county of Argyle. (Early Kings, I, p. 39.)

[4] Oswald, king of Northumbria, sojourned with the Scots in his youth. On becoming king, he sent to them for a missionary. The illustrious Aidan responded,

Kenneth, on his accession to the throne of the united Picts and Scots, was met by three foes—the Britons in Strathclyde, the Danes, and the Saxons living in the region of the Tweed. He made an alliance with the Britons by marrying his daughter to Cu, prince of Strathclyde. The government of this province thus passed to a Scoto-British prince on the death of Cu.[1] Kenneth and his successors had need of all the strength they could command. Scotland, like England, felt the force of invasion from the continent. A process of redistribution of population, which had been started by the waves of the great migrations, was still going on. The bloody wars of Charles the Great with the Saxons drove them out in crowds. The outward pressure of his policy of aggrandizement, and that of others who imitated his example, set in motion great masses of piratical sea-rovers. The conquests of the Norwegian state early in the tenth century and the establishment of a strong government multiplied the number of the pirates, who hovered, like birds of prey, on every coast. Of these Scotland received her share, and the influences thus exerted and the needs created may have had something to do in determining the relations between her and her southern neighbor.

and established a second Iona at Lindisfarne. On the battle of Degsastan *cf.* W. Malmes., I, p. 47; Bedae, Hist. Eccl., p. 88; A. S. Chron., Ad an.

[1] After 908 A. D. (Early Kings, I, pp. 54, 55.)

CHAPTER I.

THE "GREAT COMMENDATION," HAS IT AN HISTORICAL BASIS?

Did Constantine II sustain a feudal relation to Edward the Elder? is the question which greets one on the very threshold of this discussion, "the most important point in the whole dispute," "the primary fact from which the English controversialist starts," "the root of the whole matter." The so-called "commendation" of Constantine to Edward forms the first great precedent in a long line of precedents, on which the English claims to a feudal overlordship in Scotland are based. "As long as the fact of the great commendation is admitted, the case of the West Saxon Emperors of Britain stands firm."[1]

<small>Constantine II, 900–943 A. D.
Edward the Elder, 901–925.
Athelstan, 925–940</small>

Are there, then, authentic historical sources on which to base a belief that Constantine did thus "commend" himself, in such a feudal sense as to make this act a precedent, good in law, on which to found true feudal claims?

The sole authority for this act, so momentous for future ages, is the Anglo-Saxon Chronicle. The record is found "not in a ballad, or in a saga, not in the inflated rhetoric of a Latin charter, but in the honest English of the Winchester Chronicle." "No passage," says Mr. Green, "has been more fiercely fought over than this, since the legists of the English Court made it the groundwork of the claims which the English crown advanced on the allegiance of Scotland."[2] The Chronicle covers the period from the invasion of Britain by Julius Caesar to the accession of Henry II, in 1154. Together with Beda's "Ecclesiastical History" it forms the basis for the later chroniclers. The MSS., of which there are six, are considered

<small>Sources</small>

---

[1] Freeman, Norman Conq., I, Note G.

[2] Norman Conq., I, note G; Green, Conquest of England, p. 208, note.

to have been based on a common original. In MS. A., the *Corpus Christi*, the first original hand ends with the year 891 A. D., "whence it is continued in a variety of hands." "It contains many interlineary additions, apparently of the 12th Century." This copy has the following:

In this year [924] before Midsummer, King Eadweard went with a force to Nottingham, and commanded the burgh to be built on the south side of the river, opposite to the other; and the bridge over the Trent, betwixt the two burghs; and then went thence into Peakland, to Bakewell, and commanded a burgh to be built and manned there in the immediate neighborhood. And then the King of Scots and all the nation of the Scots, and Ragnald, and the sons of Eadulf, and all those who dwell in Northumbria, as well English as Danish and Northmen, and others, and also the king of the Strathclyde Welsh, and all the Strathclyde Welsh, chose him for father and lord.

MS. B. comes down to 977 A. D. "It is written in one uniform hand, apparently of the latter part of the 10th Century," and has no reference to the event of 924.

MS. C. reaches 1066 A. D., "written apparently in the same hand to 1046 A. D." No mention of the great gathering of 924.

MS. D. extends a little further than the other two—to 1079, being "written in one hand to 1016 A. D., afterwards in several . . . . It sometimes enlarges the text, not only by fuller extracts from Beda, but by the addition of many events, *relating especially to Mercia and Northumberland*." Yet it is absolutely silent regarding any great commendation.

MS. E. "The hand as well as the ink vary but little to 1122, whence to A. D. 1154, where it ends, mutilated, it is in various hands." It has no mention of the act of 924.

MS. F. to A. D. 1056, in Saxon, "is in a hand apparently of the 12th Century, and nearly of the same character throughout. It is often carelessly written, has many erasures, and is sometimes illegible, in which state it ends." It has the following:

In this year [924] King Eadweard was chosen for father and for lord by the King of Scots, and by the Scots, and by King Ragnald, and by all the Northumbrians, and also by the King of the Strathclyde Welsh, and by all the Strathclyde Welsh.[1]

These entries in two of the MSS. of the Chronicle form the sole foundation for the feudal superstructure which later generations essayed to rear. Of these MSS. one is confessedly unreliable and comes from the hands of a writer living after the Norman Conquest — probably in the twelfth century. The other is in two principal parts, one section closing with the year 891 A. D., the other being by various writers of a much later date. Mr. Green says, regarding the entry of 924:

> Nor is there, indeed, ground for placing the compilation of this section of the Chronicle of Winchester earlier than 975, or the end of Eadgar's reign, some fifty years after the "commendation" (Earle, Introd. pp. xix–xxii); and as the "imperial" claims of the English crown seem to date pretty much from the later days of Eadgar or the beginning of Aethelred's reign, an entry made at that time would naturally take its form from them.[2]

Objections to Traditional View

This MS. also has many interlineary additions, apparently of the twelfth century. There is, therefore, reasonable ground for expecting to find in this record, and on this mooted point, erroneous or fraudulent entries, and the "honest Anglo-Saxon" of the Chronicle, as well as the "inflated rhetoric of a Latin charter," will bear the closest inspection. For among the four MSS. which are ignorant of any great "commendation" is the one which is especially rich in events relating to *Mercia* and *Northumberland*.

What are the reasons, then, for doubting, in whole or in part, the record of 924? Here the Celtic scholarship of the author of the "Early Kings"[3] has proved of great value. His chief Celtic sources are Tighernac[4] and the Annals of Ulster, of which he says they are "at this period most accurate and trustworthy

---

[1] *Cf.* Thorpe, Introd. A.-S. Chron. (Mon. Hist. Brit., preface, p. 75.)
[2] Conquest of Eng., p. 208, note.
[3] "It is a work of deep research and ability, and Mr. Robertson has the advantage of an acquaintance with Celtic literature to which I can make no pretensions." (Freeman, Norman Conq., I, Note G.)
[4] Died 1088 A. D.

authorities in all connected with the Hy Ivar family," to which the Reginald of the Chronicle belonged. Mr. Skene also says:

The older annals [Irish] stand in a different [more trustworthy] position. Those of Tighernac, Inisfallen, and the Annals of Ulster, are extremely valuable for the history of Scotland.[1]

Mr. Robertson shows that the Ragnall, or Reginald, of the Chronicle was a member of the Hy Ivar family of Northmen, who appear to have come to England and Scotland by way of Ireland. At the beginning of the tenth century the most powerful among these pagan leaders were the grandsons of Ivar, who, being driven from Dublin after it was captured by the Irish King Malfinan in 902 A. D., sought to establish themselves in Scotland. In 904 they were expelled by Constantine II. Ten years later Reginald, having developed strength, was victorious over a rival in a contest off the Isle of Man. His followers rapidly increase in numbers. He lands at Waterford in 917, while his brother Sihtric threatens the coast of Leinster. Between them they regain their power over their old dependency of Dublin. The next year Reginald prepares to assert his right to Northumbria, as heir of his Danish kinsman Halfdan. When he landed among these northern Danes, he found them ready allies in an attack on York, which he took, dividing among his followers the lands of St. Cuthbert and others. Edred, Aldred of Bamborough, and his brother Uchtred, abandoning the lands they had possessed, appealed to Constantine, king of Scots, for aid. This resulted in their alliance in the first battle of Corbridge-on-Tyne, or Tynemoor, in which Reginald gained a doubtful victory. A second battle at Corbridge left him master of the field. After his death in 921 (An. Ult. 920) his brother Sihtric remained king of Northumbria. Reginald, therefore, could not have commended himself to Edward the Elder in 924 A. D.

This question is one of the greatest difficulty, as the chronology of the period is almost hopelessly confused by the English chroniclers. The value of the contemporary Irish historians is apparent. Besides these, the next best authority is probably

[1] Celtic Scotland, I, p. 25.

Simeon of Durham, whose monastery had suffered at the hands of the Dane. His work was compiled after the Conquest, and the dates are often confused or entirely wanting.[1] It was based on the A.-S. Chronicle and a copy of an old Northumbrian chronicle, known only through Simeon's work, and certain passages common to him and the A.-S. Chronicle.[2] "It is so much more circumstantial than the A.-S. Chronicle on northern events, and its chronology, as I shall hope to show presently, is so much sounder than that of the Chronicle that we can hardly be wrong in making it the original store."[3] Simeon also used as a basis for parts of his work the *Chronicon ex Chronicis* of Florence of Worcester, "next after Beda and the Saxon Chronicle the principal source of English history." It supplements the work of Marianus Scotus in the earlier parts, with references to Beda, the Saxon Chronicle, and Asser's "Life of Alfred."

Though Florence translates the Saxon Chronicle . . . . his narrative is in several instances much more circumstantial than any to be found in the existing mss. of that record, from which he also not unfrequently deviates in dates, particularly in his relation of events during the reign of Edward the Elder and Edward the Confessor. Whence it seems probable that he had before him a copy of the Chronicle varying from any now extant.

He translates as follows:

Eo tempore, rex Scottorum cum tota gente sua, Reginoldus rex Danorum cum Anglis et Danis Northanhymbriam incolentibus, rex etiam Streatcledwalorum cum suis, regem Eadwardum Seniorem sibi in patrem et dominum elegerunt, firmumque cum eo foedus pepigerunt.[4]

He assigns this event to the year 921 A. D.

Simeon states that Tilred, the successor of Cutheard, bishop of St. Cuthbert's, was in the seventh year of his episcopate when Athelstan, "suscepta regni gubernacula gloriosissime rexit.'

---

[1] Sim. Dun., Hist. Dun. Eccl., I, pp. 72, 74; Hist. de St. Cuth., I, p. 208; De Mir. et Trans., I, p. 238; Hist. Reg., II, pp. xl, 93, 123. See also Innes' Essay, Ap. 3, and War of the Gaedhill with the Gaill, Introd., specially pp. lxxxiv ff.

[2] Gesta veterum Northanhymbrorum (?).

[3] Stubbs, Rog. Hoveden, Preface, p. xxvii.

[4] Thorpe, Introd. Flor. Wig., pp. vi, vii. Also An. 921. Florence died 1118 A. D.

He also says that the taking of York, the first battle of Corbridge, and the division of the lands of St. Cuthbert among Reginald's followers had all occurred while Cutheard was bishop.[1] He alone mentions the death of Reginald (prior to his account of the death of Edward the Elder), but has a greater interest in the fact that the pagan Dane carried nothing away with him but his sins, than in the exact date of his death. He uses the expression "*tandem.*" From other sources it is certain he died in 920 or 921,[2] and, therefore, could not have taken the part assigned him in 924 by the Chronicle.

It cannot be denied that there was at this period in Ireland and Northumbria a Reginald—not of any family in general, but of the Ivar family, a great Danish leader and king, who passed back and forth with a fleet between Ireland and Scotland; that he had brothers, Godfrey and Sihtric; that a Godfrey succeeded Reginald in Ireland, and a Sihtric as king in Northumbria, both by the year 921, both of the Ivar family. It cannot be doubted that Reginald made an expedition across the channel and took York by storm before the year 923, assigned to that event in the Chronicle. There is no evidence that he lost or retook York at this period. It is highly improbable that there should have been two men of the same name and family and age, whose careers should have been thus identical. That part of the Chronicle, therefore, which affirms the taking of York in 923 and the commendation of Reginald in 924 must be in error, since it conflicts with these undoubted facts, shown by the

---

[1] Sim. Dun., Hist. Dun. Eccl., I, p. 74. Cutheard's predecessor, Eardulf, died in the same year with King Alfred (901). Cutheard died "cum jam quintum decimum suo in episcopatu ageret annum." Then Tilred succeeded. There is evident error in the chronology, since Edward the Elder was, according to this, still reigning in Tilred's seventh year. But the taking of York by Reginald could not have been in 923, the date assigned by the Chronicle, and probably not later than 918, since it occurred during the life of Cutheard.

[2] "The entry [A.-S. Chron. 924] cannot be contemporary, for Reginald, whom it makes king in Northumbria, had died three years before, in 921." (Green, Conquest of England, p. 208.) Mr. Skene expresses the opinion "that Mr. Freeman has failed, on the whole, to meet Mr. Robertson's criticism" regarding the death of Reginald, and the bearing of this passage on the commendation of the Scot king to Edward the Elder. (Celtic Scotland, I, p. 350.)

comparative testimony of the other early sources. It cannot, therefore, be made a basis for argument.[1]

A similar instance of error or fraud occurs in two charters of Athelstan of the year 930 A. D.,[2] in which the signature of Reginald appears. These are both marked by Kemble as untrustworthy, and are given up by Freeman.

But there are other grounds on which to question the correctness of this statement of the Chronicle. It implies (1) a meeting at Bakewell in Peakland, and not at some other place and time; (2) a meeting of the *people* as well as of their kings. Mr. Freeman seeks to maintain (1) that this gathering did not necessarily occur at Bakewell, nor at this specific time; (2) that the English king did not become the personal lord of each man, but of the kings, or chiefs, only.[3] In reply it may be said (1) that the chronicler would hardly have followed the course of Edward's military expeditions so explicitly as he has done throughout his reign, only to break down at the most important point in his last year. There is, moreover, not a particle of evidence for any advance beyond Bakewell, or of a meeting at any other time than this. (2) It is evident from the history of Edward's reign, and from the opinion of later writers, that such acts of submission took place in the immediate neighborhood of the people concerned (including both people and leaders), or in the later period, in the case of kings, on the borders between the two kingdoms. The following are illustrations:

King Eadweard went with some of his force to Maldon in Essex, and there encamped, while the burgh at Witham was being wrought and built; and a good deal of the folk submitted to him, who were before under the power of the Danish men.

King Eadweard went with his force to Buckingham. . . . And Thurkytel jarl sought him for his lord, and all the holds,[4] and almost

---

[1] Mr. Freeman admits that "a scribe might easily put Reagnald instead of some other name," thus admitting the force of the argument. (N. C., I, Note G.) On similar errors in Chronicle see Cod. Dip., I, p. lxxxv.

[2] Cod. Dip., II, Nos. 351, 352.

[3] Norman Conq., I, Note G. *Per contra cf.* Green, Conq. of Eng., p. 208.

[4] A.-S. Chron., An. 905, Note 4.

all the chief men of Bedford, and also many of those belonging to Northampton.

King Eadweard went with an army to Bedford . . . . and gained the burgh; and almost all the townsmen who had previously dwelt there turned to him.

King Eadweard, with a force of West Saxons, went to Passenham, and sat there while they surrounded the burgh at Towcester with a stone wall. And Thurferth jarl, and the holds, and all the army which belonged to Northampton, north as far as the Welland, submitted to him and sought him for their lord and protector . . . . and all the folk that were left there [Huntingdon] of the peasantry submitted to King Eadweard and sought his peace and protection. . . .

Eadweard, with an army of West Saxons, went to Colchester . . . . and a great number of people submitted to him, both in East Anglia and in Essex, who had before been under the power of the Danes. And all the army in East Anglia swore unity with him, that they all that would that he would, and would protect all that the king would protect both by sea and by land. And the army which belonged to Cambridge chose him specially for their lord and protector and confirmed it by oaths as he it then dictated.

Eadweard went with a force to Stamford, and commanded the burgh to be wrought on the south side of the river; and all the people who belonged to the northern burgh submitted to him and sought him for their lord. . . . He took possession of the burgh at Tamworth, and all the people in the Mercians land, who had before been subject to Aethelflaed, submitted to him. And the kings of the North Welsh, Howel, Cleduac, and Jeothwell, and all the North Welsh race, sought him for lord. He then went to Nottingham, and reduced the burgh, and ordered it to be repaired and peopled, both with Englishmen and Danish. And all the people who were settled in the Mercians land submitted to him, both Danish and English.

Athelstan in like manner received the submission of the North Welsh at Hereford and of the Cornishmen at Exeter.[1]

These instances, which might be multiplied, show what was the universal custom of that age. The king went from place to place, fortifying and strengthening defenses, and received the submission and oaths of allegiance of the people in

---

[1] A.-S. Chron., An. 913, 915, 919, 921, 922; W. Malmes., Gest. Reg., I, p. 148.

groups, which gathered from the country centering on the places where he was. Each freeman swore to be faithful and true to his Saxon "Hlaford and Mundbora." This would render it imperative that the place of meeting should be centrally located, and not so far removed but that the distant freemen could be present without serious hardship or delay. It is interesting to note the *number* of places at which Edward received the submission of his people.[1] But Bakewell in Peakland is in Derbyshire, on the border of Edward's dominions, and far removed from Strathclyde and distant Scotland. The idea of these peoples going thither to do homage is completely at variance with the customs and history of this period. Writers of a later age testify what they conceive the earlier custom to have been. The kings met, if at all, on the borders of the two kingdoms,[2] and such a meeting was usually supported by the march of an English army into the north. It is noteworthy that in all Simeon's work drawn from *original* sources there is not the slightest trace of any act of submission to Edward the Elder on the part of the people of the north. He writes of the troubles with the Danes, of the alliance which the Scottish king headed against them, of the life and death of Reginald and of King Edward. But he is profoundly ignorant of any union of these foes and of the gathering of their hosts at Bakewell before their feudal lord. Is it likely such an event, affecting the north so radically, could have occurred and escaped absolutely the notice of the northern, Irish, and Danish chroniclers? He shows his conception of the matter when he says of Athelstan: "*primusque regum* totius Britanniae quaqua versum adeptus imperium."[3]

Summary   The only authority, then, for the so-called "commendation" is the passage cited from the Winchester MS. of the A.-S. Chronicle. Of the first part of the entry there is no doubt. It is in perfect accord with the narrative of the rest of Edward's reign in its language, in the mode of action, and in its

---

[1] A careful comparison of the Chronicle with Droysen, or some good atlas, is helpful.
[2] Fl. Wig., and Sim. Dun., An. 1092.
[3] *Cf.* Ritson, Annals of Picts, etc., An. 937.

particularistic character. This is especially noteworthy. There is good cause for believing that the original entry closed with the words "immediate neighborhood," though it may have included the submission of the Danes living near the Peak in Derbyshire. Some such entry seems to have been enlarged by the later writers to support the claims of a feudal age. For now the narrative suddenly abandons its old character, becomes universal rather than particular, violates all its precedents as to custom, and uses an expression nowhere again found in the history of the reigns of Alfred, Edward, or Athelstan.[1]

And then the King of Scots and all the nation of the Scots, and Ragnald, and the sons of Eadulf, and all those who dwell in Northumbria, as well English as Danish and Northmen, *and others*, and also the King of the Strathclyde Welsh, and all the Strathclyde Welsh, chose him for *father* and for lord.

Everywhere else the words are either "*hlaforde and mundbora*," "lord and protector," or simply "hlaforde." By its very universality the statement overreaches itself. It bears on its face the stamp of exaggeration and fabrication which characterizes the narratives of the reign of Edgar. Nor is the phenomenon difficult to explain in the light of the fact that he endowed no less than forty-eight religious houses.[2] It is certainly contradicted by the fact that Reginald died before the year 924. If 921, the date given by Florence, be accepted, it involves a worse quandary, for it leaves the last three, and most important, years of Edward's reign a blank.[3] It is inconsistent with the desperate struggle which Athelstan and Edmund had with the people of the north. It would not have been had they submitted *after conquest*. But that they should take the trouble *voluntarily* to go and submit to a possible, but far-distant foe, who had never entered their territories nor in any way threatened them, is beyond reason. Equally absurd, in this quest of voluntary servitude by a rugged, daring, turbulent people, is the

---

[1] Malcolm II (1005-1034) is called "Lord and *Father* of the West."
[2] Pinkerton, An Enquiry, etc., II, p. 219.
[3] Mr. Freeman rightly insists on 924 as the true date.

willing union of Constantine and his Saxon allies with the Dane Reginald, by whom they had been but recently defeated, who still held, and his brother Sihtric after him, the northern kingdom he and his followers had won.

The conclusion is inevitable. At his death Alfred was king "over all the Angle race except the part that was under the dominion of the Danes."[1] His son Edward pushed out the bounds of the kingdom on the north to the Peak of Derbyshire. But the submission of the *Northumbrian* Danes did not occur till the death of Sihtric, under the reign of Athelstan. The story of the great "commendation" of the north to Edward cannot, therefore, be accepted as an historical fact.

King Edward the Elder died in 925 A. D., and left to his son Athelstan the work of consolidating and extending the kingdom. The historical records of his glorious reign are scanty, and largely based on traditions and legends, old poems, and sagas—materials which, literally translated or adopted into the Latin of the writers of a feudal age, did not lose in power to enhance the glories of an English king. Constantine II was in the midst of his long reign, and Sihtric, the brother of Reginald the Dane, was king in Northumbria. Malmesbury speaks of him as one "qui . . . . antecessorum regum potentiam rugatis naribus derisisset"[2]—a striking commentary on the supposed voluntary submission to Edward the Elder, of which, however, Malmesbury was ignorant. These words indicate that the Northumbrian Danes did not submit to a Saxon overlord till Athelstan's day. He courted the alliance of Sihtric by giving him his sister in marriage. Doubtless he saw here an opportunity to gain a legal claim on the Northumbrian possessions, which was indeed afforded him on Sihtric's death soon after, in 927 A. D. The names of the Danish earls now first appear in the authentic charters of Athelstan.[3]

Athelstan, 925–940 A. D.

His Relations to Northumbria

[1] A.-S. Chron., An. 901. [2] Wm. Malmes., Gesta Reg., I, p. 146.
[3] Robertson, Early Kings, Ap. L; Cod. Dip., Nos. 353, 363.

and Scotland

One MS., only, of the A.-S. Chronicle relates any meeting between Athelstan and Constantine, the king of Scots. It reads:

And Sihtric died; and Athelstan assumed the kingdom of the Northumbrians; [and he subjugated all the kings who were in this island; first, Howel king of the West Welsh, and Constantine king of the Scots, and Owen king of Gwent, and Ealdred, son of Ealdulf of Bamborough:] and with pledge and with oaths they confirmed peace, in the place which is named Eâmôt [Emmet in Yorkshire?] .... and renounced every kind of idolatry; and after that departed in peace.

William of Malmesbury also represents Constantine and Eugenius, king of Strathclyde, as coming to Athelstan at Dacor, in Cumberland, to surrender their kingdoms to him; by whose order, also, Constantine's son is baptized.[1] The confusion here between pagan Danes and Christian Scots who renounce idolatry, is apparent, nor is it in accord with the fact that Constantine, some years before, had presided over a church council at Scone. If, however, as Mr. Robertson suggests, that portion of the Chronicle in brackets be omitted, the sense will be at once restored. It seems to be an interpolation, and certainly shows the chronicler was in error.[2] Malmesbury is in the same confusion. It is quite probable that the Dane Sihtric renounced idolatry when he married Athelstan's sister, and that his son Olave, who ended his days in the monastery of Iona,[3] was baptized through the agency of the English king. "As neither Constantine nor Eogan ever appear in the character of *subreguli*, the first part of the story may be dismissed as an exaggeration, the supposed paganism of [Constantine] throwing great suspicion on the remainder." This is only one instance of the way in which Scots and Danes are recklessly confused as the common subjects of the English crown.[4]

[1] Gesta Reg., I, p. 147; A.-S. Chron., An. 926. (Cott. Tiber., B. IV.)

[2] Haddan and Stubbs, Counc., II, p. 144; A. D. 906. *Cf.* Ritson, An. of Picts, etc., II, p. 79. Constantinus rex et Cellachus episcopus, leges disciplinasque fidei, atque jura ecclesiarum evangelorumque. ... in colle credulitatis prope regali civitati Scoan devoverunt custoditur [custodiri]. (Skene, Celtic Scot., I, p. 351.)

[3] In 980 A. D. *Cf.* Early Kings, I, p. 74. [4] Early Kings, I, p. 60; II, p. 397.

Sihtric left a son, Olave, or Anlaf, who fled to Ireland, being too young to oppose Athelstan. At a later time Olave became Constantine's son-in-law, and it is this alliance which first excited Athelstan's suspicion and hostility. An English army wasted the land, while a fleet swept the coasts, preventing the junction of Irish and Scottish forces. The Chronicle reads :

Athelstan went into Scotland with both a land force and a ship force, and ravaged a great part of it.

This is given in all the MSS. now published, but there is not a word which can be twisted to imply any submission, or anything on which a feudal claim might be based. Anglo-Norman writers magnified this into a complete subjugation of Scotland, but the battle of Brunanburh is evidence to the contrary. It was rather a military and naval demonstration to prevent the union of forces hostile to the English king. There is no record of any actual contest at this time.[1]

Brunanburh The battle of Brunanburh, just mentioned, occurred in 937 A. D., probably in a place some distance south of the Humber, and near the Trent. Here a great host met to fight for dominion in Northumbria. Athelstan and his Saxon and Danish forces were aided by the "pagan rovers of the German Ocean." And it is to these Norsemen that

[1] A.-S. Chron., An. 933; Celtic Scotland, I, p. 352.
Mr. Robertson (Early Kings, I, p. 62) calls attention to the three versions which Simeon gives of this event. (Hist. Dun. Eccl., I, p. 74, Hist. Reg., II, p. 124.) The first, from original sources, mentions only the extent of the incursion to Dunfoeder (or Forteviot) and Wertermore, the fleet reaching the coast of Caithness; the second, which copies Florence of Worcester, represents Constantine as purchasing peace by giving his son as a hostage; the third, in recognition of the gifts of Athelstan to the shrine of St. Cuthbert, declares Scotland to be thoroughly subdued. "According to Brompton (Twysden, p. 838), Athelstan demanded a sign from St. John of Beverly 'quo praesentes et futuri cognoscere possent Scotos de jure debere Anglis subjugari.' It was granted, and the king's sword clove an ell of rock from the foundations of Dunbar Castle! 'Possessiones, privilegia, et libertates,' rewarded the miracle, a price for which there was scarcely a patron saint in the country who would not have been made to confirm with signs and wonders the rightful supremacy of the English king over any people he chose to name. The monks of Newburgh outdid even Brompton, detaining Athelstan for three years in Scotland, whilst he placed 'princes' over her provinces, provosts over her cities, and settled the amount of tribute to be paid from the most distant islands!"

the saga attributes the victory. Opposed to them was a mixed force led by Constantine, king of Scots; it included his son-in-law, Olave Sitricson; Olave, the son of Godfrey, from Ireland; and Eogan, king of Strathclyde, who also was a kinsman of Constantine. The strife was terrific, the slaughter frightful, the victory of the English king glorious. The clang and roar of the battle still resound in the ancient war song with which the Chronicle celebrates the valor of the heroes of that day. It left Athelstan the undoubted master of Northumbria, and spread his fame far among the royal courts of the continent. But there is no evidence that he pursued his retreating enemy into the north, or made terms with them. Nor indeed was there reason for it, since he had gained his object — the defeat of the powers that threatened his supremacy in Northumbria. It should be borne in mind that this was an agressive war on the part of the allies of the north — probably on English soil south of the Humber.

The exact site of Brunanburh is one of the unsolved problems of history. Nor is it possible to reach more than an inferential conclusion with the sources at present available. Johnstone and Spruner have located it in the extreme limits of Northumbria, just south of the Tweed. Others advocate a site in Lancashire, to explain the flight of Anlaf, son of Godfrey, after his defeat — "o'er the deep water, Dublin to seek." Capgrave says a battle between Athelstan, Anlaf, king of Ireland, and Constantine, king of Scots, occurred at Bamborough; but as he did not write till the fifteenth century, and adds the pleasing information that "thorow the prayeres of Seynt Ode, a swerd fel fro Hevene into his [Athelstan's] schaberk," his testimony is not of the highest value.[1] The original authorities are the A.-S. Chronicle, Florence of Worcester, and Simeon of Durham. The poem in the Chronicle clearly indicates that a large part of the hostile forces *came* and *departed* by sea (the Humber and the Forth — not the Tweed — were the great gateways for the entrance of invading

Its Site

---

[1] Chron. Eng., p. 117.

hordes into England and Scotland). But Florence is more explicit, and the later writers follow him almost without exception. As he had a copy of the A.-S. Chronicle not now extant, his authority is of the very first order. He distinctly says that Anlaf, king of Ireland and of many islands, incited by his ally and father-in-law, Constantine, king of the Scots, entered the *mouth* of the Humber with a powerful fleet, and that Athelstan and his brother Edmund met them at a place called Brunanburh.[1] One of the accounts given in Simeon relates that the battle was fought at Weondune, which is also called Etbrunnanwerc, or Brunnanbyrig,[2] and that Anlaf had a fleet of six hundred and fifteen ships. The other account follows Florence without comment. Hoveden combines the accounts of Florence and Simeon, bringing the large fleet into England through the Humber. There seems no doubt, therefore, that the battle occurred somewhere within easy reach of the Humber, since the enemy not only entered thence, but fled in their ships after their defeat. Droysen prefers the spot in Lincolnshire already referred to. Mr. Skene considers that Aldborough, situated on the Ouse, a little northwest of York, and accessible by water from the Humber, best fulfills the conditions required for the site of Brunanburh. His chief objection to a location further south is, that if a large part of the allied forces came from the north by land, it is unlikely that Athelstan would have permitted them to penetrate so far into his dominions without giving them battle. But, granting that they came thus, the objection does not seem valid. The region north of the Humber, and even Lincolnshire, was still distinctly Danish in race and sympathy. Among the numerous burhs built by Edward the Chronicle does not mention one in Lincoln. The northern extent of his power was apparently limited by Stamford on the Welland, by Nottingham, the Peak in Derbyshire, and Manchester. So that, in reality, Athelstan's distinctive kingdom had not been touched nor scarcely threatened till the allied forces reached the Humber. The movement from the north was a serious menace to his

---

[1] Fl. Wig., I, p. 132.   [2] Etbrunnanmere (Skene).

power—a menace which was carried into effect when the Danes wrested from his brother Edmund half the kingdom. The originator of a wise policy might well hesitate in the presence of this organized effort to check the extension of English supremacy beyond the Humber. He would seek to draw the allies as far as possible from their base of supplies, to make the attack against them with all the forces of the kingdom thoroughly organized, and, if possible, on English soil, rather than in the midst of the hostile north. Malmesbury suggests just this process. Anlaf Sitricson "spe invadendi regni . . . . terminos transierat;" "multum in Angliam processerat juvenis audacissimus." He apologizes for Athelstan's apparent dilatoriness on the ground that he had purposely retreated, in order to derive greater honor from conquering his furious assailants. The Norse sagas also intimate that all the country beyond the Humber was in a turmoil, and that the two earls set up by Athelstan had been driven out. It is not out of place, therefore, to look for this battlefield south of the Humber. While Aldbourough doubtless formed a convenient "trysting place," accessible alike from the Humber, the north, and the west, a vital objection to it is the comparative ease with which Athelstan and his army might have blocked the waterway which furnished the line of retreat for the Danish fleet of six hundred and fifteen ships. This objection does not hold against the site in Lincolnshire. It also was accessible from the north and west. The people were akin to the invaders. At the same time it had such an intimate connection with the English kingdom that Athelstan could easily approach it, or at need fall back on his more loyal subjects. It was an ideal choice for the invaders. On the east was the sea, to the west the Trent, while in the rear their fleet could lie at anchor in the Humber or the Trent. A Roman road, crossing Watling street at right angles, connected the lands of the Mercians and West-Saxons (who figure in the poem on Brunanburh) with Lincoln ; another, starting at London, passed through Lincoln and on to the Humber; still another crossed the Trent above Lincoln, affording easy communication with Chester and the important centers in the extreme north and west. Here, then, the great hosts met to cast the lot of battle for supremacy in Northumbria. From dawn to twilight the West-Saxons "followed the footsteps of the hostile nations." Congenial it was to Edward's offspring that they "'gainst every foe, should *the land defend, treasure and homes.*" Nor did they rest till the great host was dispersed in flight by sea and land, or "by swords laid to sleep" on that famous battle-stead. There can be no doubt that this was an aggressive movement on the part of the allies for the recovery of the Northumbrian districts which Athelstan had annexed to his kingdom on the death of Sihtric. Athelstan was on the defensive, and the site in Lincolnshire assigned by Droysen as the scene of this famous battle seems most reasonable and practicable. It certainly was in the immediate vicinity of the Humber.[1]

Athelstan, having now secured himself on the north, turned to Wales and determined the regular tribute which the Welsh kings should pay to their Saxon overlord.[2] Their names, under the title of *subreguli*, first appear, together with those of the Danish leaders, in the charters of Athelstan. Welsh bishops eventually become suffragans of the archbishop of Canterbury, and the English king is the common lawmaker and defender of Welsh, Danes, and English alike.[3] But the name of the king of Scots does not

Athelstan in Wales

---

[1] *Cf.* A.-S. Chron. and Hoveden, An. 937; Sim. Dun., I, p. 76; II, pp. xxxiii, 125; Skene, Celtic Scot., I, pp. 352 ff.; Malmes., Gesta Reg., I, p. 142; *The Contemp. Review*, Nov., 1876; Guest, Origines Celticae, II, p. 218.

[2] Walt. of Cov., whose unreliability has already been commented on, puts into Athelstan's mouth the words, "Gloriosus est regem facere quam regem esse." *Cf.* also A.-S. Chron, An. 1063; W. Malmes., Gesta Reg., I, p. 148: Ita quod nullus ante eum rex *vel cogitare praesumpserat*, ipse in effectum formavit, ut ei nomine Vectigalis annuatim vigenti libras auri, trecentas argenti, penderent, boves viginti quinque milia annumerent, etc.

[3] *Cf.* Robertson, Early Kings, II, p. 393; Cod. Dip., Nos. 353, 363, 364, 411, 426, 433, 451; Thorpe, I, p. 275, Laws of Edgar: "Let this ordinance be common to all the people, whether English, Danes, or Britons, *on every side of my dominions.*" This does not include the Scots. Makower says: "As regards Wales in particular, the princes of that country fell, from the beginning of the 9th century, into political

appear in any authentic charter, as an attesting *subregulus*; the church is notably independent of English control; and from the days of Oswy and Egfrid to the time of Henry II, no tribute is levied on the kingdom of the Scots, nor is there any supervision exercised by an English king in its internal affairs. Stronger proofs of an independent kingdom could scarcely be produced.

dependence on the Anglo-Saxon kings. Soon afterwards began the gradual coalescence of the constitutions of the two churches. The bishoprics of South Wales came, from the end of the 9th century, into more or less close connection with the Anglo-Saxon church. But it was not until the beginning of the 12th century that the Welsh bishops completed their submission to the Archbishop of Canterbury, and still another century passed before Welsh independence in state and church was wholly overthrown." (Constit. Hist. Ch. of Eng., p. 6.) *Cf.* also Haddan and Stubbs, Counc., I, pp. 202–620.

CHAPTER II.

THE CESSIONS OF CUMBERLAND AND LOTHIAN.

On the death of Athelstan, his successor, Edmund (940-946 A. D.) was unable to hold together the kingdom which his brother had conquered. The Danes of Northumbria rose in revolt, and again called in the two Olaves. It is not known what part, if any, Constantine took. His increasing old age would be a good reason for his non-participation in the movement. This time the victory rested with the rebels. Eric, the son of Harold Harfager, was driven from Northumbria,[1] and all Athelstan's dominions north of Watling street were ceded to the two Olaves. It required years of hard fighting to bring the Danelagh again to submission, but in 944 A. D. Northumbria was forced to yield. Edmund then turned his arms against Cumberland. He

Accession of Edmund. Reduction of the Danelagh

.... harried over all Cumberland and gave it all up to Malcolm [I] King of Scots on the condition that he should be his co-operator both on sea and land.

The later chroniclers add nothing essential to this record, except to give it a feudal coloring by translating *midwyrhta*, "fellow-workman," as *fidelis*.[2]

It is difficult to determine just what "Cumbraland" meant in Edmund's day. Mr. Freeman says, "I wish to keep myself as clear as possible from all mazes as to the ever fluctuating boundaries of Strathclyde and Cumberland."

"Cumbraland"

But he does not hesitate to declare that Edmund conquered and *abolished the kingdom of Strathclyde*, conferring part

---

[1] He had threatened the northern coasts of England soon after the battle of Brunanburh. Athelstan was perhaps unwilling to undertake another conflict of arms so soon, or desired to "fight fire with fire." Hence he secured the alliance of Eric by giving into his care the disputed territory.

[2] A.-S. Chron., An. 945. Four MSS. have this record. Two mention only the

of it, under the name of Cumberland on Malcolm by the "usual tenure of faithful service in war."[1] Mr. Freeman has no authority for this statement. The chronicles he cites use the term Cumberland, or Cumbria. His statement implies that Strathclyde and Cumberland were the same, which is the very point at issue, and in regard to which he adduces no proof. Mr. Robertson shows that at one time the name Cumbria, or Cumberland, was applied to a wide territory extending at least from Dumbarton to North Wales. This was gradually reduced by the additions made to Northumbria, by the grants of Egfrid to St. Cuthbert, taking in the modern Cumberland and Westmoreland, and by the settlements of the Angles in Candida Casa. There can be no doubt that the natural tendency would be in favor of a gradual division of the extensive Cumbria of the earlier period into two parts, one English, the other Scotch, the dividing line being one of nature's own making—the Solway. This accords perfectly with the history of this region, so far as it is known, and is borne out by the fact that the term Cumberland is still applied to the region south of the Solway, while Scottish Cumbria, or Strathclyde, lost its title eventually and was united (about 1018 A. D.) with the northern kingdom. But it remained as a semi-independent kingdom under the control of a branch of the MacAlpin family from the opening of the tenth century to the reign of Malcolm II (1005–1034 A. D.) English Cumbria was probably under the Northumbrian earls, or in a state of anarchy. With its numerous lakes and its situation on the northwest coast, it formed an admirable retreat for the pirate fleets from Ireland and the islands. And it was doubtless of this nest of intruders that

Ceded to Malcolm I Edmund made havoc, delivering the province over to Malcolm (943–954 A. D.), on condition that he should defend it, as his ally, by sea and land.[2] Had Malcolm been a vassal of the English crown, there would have

expedition to the north. *Cf.* Rog. Wend., Flor. Hist., I, p. 500, with Robertson, Early Kings, I, p. 70, note.

[1] Norman Conq., I, Note H., p. 62; William Rufus, II, p. 545.

[2] Early Kings, I, p. 70.

been no need to purchase his alliance at such a price. It is noteworthy that there is here no intimation of any previous relations such as this, nor of any service due as of right from the king of Scots to the king of the English because of previous acts or compacts. It is only after this time that references to precedents occur, viz., when feudal ideas take shape and a legal basis is sought for feudal claims. Then it is that the language of the ordinary incidents of victory and defeat, of submission or alliance, are translated into feudal terms, and interpreted in a way that the actors in those events little dreamed of. The compact with Malcolm was for his lifetime, as will appear presently, and there is no intimation in the writers before the feudal age that his successors were involved in any way. When Edmund died in 946 A. D., the compact was renewed with Eadred. Mr. Freeman says: "That the Scots renewed their oaths on the accession of Eadred is no proof of hostile feelings on either side." Malmesbury's statement that the Northumbrians and Scots made Eric their king and suffered a common punishment by Eadred again illustrates the confusion between Scot and Dane in the mind of the English monk. His statement is correct regarding the Northumbrians, but contradicts the facts of Scottish history by ignoring the kingship of Malcolm I. It entirely lacks the support of the Chronicle, which says, "Eadred harried over all Northumberland, because they had taken Eric for their king." In 954 he "assumed the kingdom of the Northumbrians," having apparently had the assistance of his Scottish allies. As there is no further mention of the "Scottish oaths," it seems clear in the light of later events that they were given in return for the grant of Cumberland, and that it was held by Malcolm I for his own lifetime only.[1]

Scots and Danes Confused

Reversion of Cumberland

A charter of Edgar's reign, dated 966 A. D., bears the signature of Kenneth, "rex Scotorum," and of Malcolm, "rex Cumbrorum." Its spurious character is noted by Mr. Kemble,

[1] A.-S. Chron., An. 946, 948, 954; W. Malmes., Gesta Reg., I, p. 162; Norman Conq., I, p. 63.

Evidences

so that it affords no proof that the Scots still held the grant of Cumberland.¹ Kenneth did not become king until five years later, 971 A. D. As for Malcolm, Mr. Robertson says:

There could have been no 'King of the Cumbrians' at this time, for the grant of *Cumberland*, made to Malcolm the First in 945, and for which he renewed his oaths upon the accession of Edred, ceased upon the death of the Scottish King, and the feudal subinfeudation of that province as a fief held by the Scottish Tanist is totally contrary to the real history of the period. Donald, son of the Eogan who appears to have fallen at Brunanburgh, was King of Strathclyde during the whole of Edgar's reign, dying in the same year as the English King, whilst on a pilgrimage to Rome ; and if the 'rex Cumbrorum' means 'King of Strathclyde,' no Malcolm could have appeared at Chester² in that capacity. Malcolm, King of the Cumbrians, is indubitably a *myth*.³

The subsequent history also conflicts with the theory that the king of Scots retained the grant of Cumberland after the death of Malcolm I. Kenneth II (971–995) on his accession "statim predavit Britanniam ex parte." He threw up earthworks at the fordable places along the Forth, and carried his ravages "ad Stammoir, ad Cluiam et ad Stang na Deram."⁴ Ethelred also "went to Cumberland and ravaged it very nigh all." No mention is made of the Scots by a single authority till John of Fordun. He seized on Cumberland as a convenient means of escaping the claims of the English chroniclers, and made it the counterpart of the later earldom of Huntingdon. He explained Ethelred's invasion on the ground that the king of the Cumbrians (?) had refused to pay his share of the Danegeld. Mr. Freeman admits Fordun is not an authority "of the first order," but does not scruple to base his argument upon his testimony. There is not a shred of evidence elsewhere to show any connection between the king of Scots and Cumberland at this

---

¹ Cod. Dip., No. 519.
² In Edgar's royal progress on the Dee.
³ Early Kings, I, pp. 72, 92, note.
⁴ Innes' Essay, Ap. 3. Stanemor is in Cumberland near its junction with Westmoreland, Northumberland, and Durham.

time. Henry of Huntingdon (An. 1000) says Ethelred went into Cumberland "*ubi maxima mansio Dacorum erat, vicitque Dacos bello maximo.*" Had either Cumberland or Lothian been held of the English crown, it can hardly be doubted that Ethelred would have demanded the Danegeld from them, and the fact would have been noted by the earlier English chroniclers.[1]

Simeon of Durham adds further proof when he describes the ravages of Malcolm III in Teesdale and up and down the coast. His army was led through Cumberland and then eastward, avoiding Northumbria. He describes the ravages of Earl Cospatric in Cumberland, and expressly states that it was under Malcolm's dominion "non jure possessa sed *violenter subjugata.*"[2] The weight of evidence is certainly against the theory that Cumberland was ontinuously held of the English king by the king of Scots as a feudal fief. Whether it was withdrawn because of Malcolm's lack of fidelity, or for other reasons, is not stated. But it is significant that this should have been the period in which Malcolm's successor, Indulf (son of Constantine II), began the extension of Scottish dominion toward the Tweed. It may well be that this was in retaliation for the withdrawal of Cumberland on the death of Malcolm I. Whatever the cause, it is certain that Indulf (954–962) invaded Lothian, and that Edinburgh, "the frontier fortress of the great Northumbrian Bretwalda," passed from English to Scottish control.[3]

Lothian

This is the first definite step toward the acquirement of Lothian. None of the early chroniclers state how the cession came about. The St. Albans chroniclers, Wendover and Wallingford, wrote not earlier than the thirteenth century. They give a minute account of how Kenneth II (991–995) was brought to Edgar, and of the arrangements by which the transfer of Lothian was accomplished. Full details

Its Cession

---

[1] A.-S. Chron., An. 1000; Early Kings, I, p. 72, note; II, pp. 186, 387; Norman Conquest, I, p. 300. Ap. H, FF. Hume bases his narrative on Fordun.

[2] Sim. Dun., Hist. Reg., pp. 190, 191.

[3] Innes Essay, Ap. 3; Freeman, Norman Conq., I, Note II.

of the feudal homage to be rendered and of the provisions for the progress of Kenneth to Edgar's court are not overlooked.

Simeon of Durham, who wrote at least a century earlier than these chroniclers, is quite ignorant of their story, and makes a very different statement. Malcolm II (1005–1034) invaded Northumbria. The old Ealdorman Waltheof shut himself in behind the walls of Bamborough. But his son Uchtred took the field and not only defeated the Scots, but decorated the walls of Durham with the heads of the slain.[1] Some years later Uchtred was murdered, and his cowardly brother Eadulf, fearing the vengeance of the Scots, ceded Lothian to them. The passage reads:

Quo [Uchtredo] occiso, frater ipsius Eadulf, cognomento Cudel, ignavus et valde et timidus ei successit in comitatum. Timens autem ne Scotti mortem suorum, quos frater ejus, ut supradictum est, occiderat, in se vindicarent, *totum* Lodoneium ob satisfactionem et firmam concordiam eis donavit. Hoc modo Lodoneium adjectum est regno Scottorum.

The editor of the Rolls Series says of the *De Obs. Dun.*:

It is an authentic though fragmentary record of the wild and miserable age of Ethelred. . . . The date of writing seems to have been about 1090.

These are the sources. The question of the cession has been fully discussed on both sides.[2] Mr. Freeman concedes

. . . . the infinite superiority of Simeon, our very best authority for Northumbrian affairs, over two late and often inaccurate writers like John of Wallingford and Roger of Wendover. . . . Simeon's statement proves that some cession of Lothian was made by Eadwulf, and if so, we can hardly be wrong in setting it down as a result of the battle of Carham. (1028 A. D.)

The stories of John and Roger, however, support Mr. Freeman's theory of the feudal dependence of Scotland on her Imperial Lord, and he, therefore, seeks with his wonted ingenuity, to weave out of them something to his purpose. But

---

[1] On the date *cf.* Sim. Dun., I, pp. 215–16 with Early Kings, I, p. 92.

[2] Sim. Dun., I, p. 218; Norman Conq., I, Note I; Early Kings, I, pp. 95, 96; II, pp. 390, 399.

the legends and fabrications which came from the hands of the later chroniclers, centering about the reign of Edgar as one of several foci, have been already referred to, and are too well known to need further characterization. The monastic writers knew no bounds when singing the praises of those who had been generous to their houses — of whom Edgar was one of the first. Richard of Cirencester says of Edgar's reign: "God helping him, he had the whole island in his hand, and Scotland, Wales, and Cumbria, gladly ran to submit themselves to him." Mr. Green says,

. . . . side by side, two, with this statelier song [of Athelstan's day], we catch glimpses of a wilder and more romantic upgrowth of popular verse, which wrapped in an atmosphere of romance the lives of kings such as Athelstan and Eadgar.

These ballads were preserved down to the twelfth century, when

. . . . they were introduced by the writers of the time into our own history much to its confusion. . . . Historically these legends stand on the same footing as the other romances embedded in Malmesbury.[1]

It is, therefore, unwarrantable to base an argument on such questionable authorities, especially when they disagree with the definite, trustworthy statement of an authority like Simeon. It is objected that in his account of the battle of Carham the English forces are represented as coming from the region between the Tees and the Tweed, and that it should have included the people of Lothian as well, if that province had not already been ceded to the king of Scots.[2] But it is only necessary to remember that the Scots took the stronghold of Edinburgh during the reign of Indulf, and had held it for some fifty years, during which they had been steadily pushing southward. Lothian thus became a border territory, harried from both sides. The march of Malcolm's host to Carham, moreover, must have

---

[1] Ric. de Cirenc., II, p. 91; Conq. of Eng., pp. 284, 310, note; W. Malmes., Gesta Reg., Ad. an., and Introd. (Stubbs), p. lxvi. Malmesbury is the first exponent of popular legend in history.

[2] Norman Conq., I, Note LLL.

caused the people of this district either to join him or to remain neutral.

Thus, either by cession through the fears of Eadulf Cudel, or by conquest, Lothian passed under the dominion of the king of Scots. It may well be asked how two feudatories could annex or resign territories without the consent, or remonstrance, of their overlord, and the whole transaction points to the fact that *Malcolm* could not have been a vassal of the English crown at this time.

Cnut

Cnut, on his return from Rome, some fourteen years later, made an expedition to the north, which may have had some reference to the transfer of Lothian. The authority for this expedition is the Chronicle, under the year 1031 A. D.:[1] "The Scots' king Malcolm submitted to him [Cnut] and became his man, but held that only a little while." This is from MS. D, which, after 1016 A. D., is written in several hands, and is especially full on events relating to Mercia and Northumberland. Two other MSS., E and F, one in the same hand to 1122 A. D., the other apparently of the twelfth century, add "and two other kings, Maelbaethe and Jehmarc." Their addition of these names and their omission of the phrase "he held that [allegiance] only a little while," render their testimony suspicious. Mr. Robertson has shown that Macbeth was not even Mormaor of Moray till the death of his kinsman Gilcomgain, in 1032.[2] In any case, the results of the meeting, on Scotland, were as transitory as the passing clouds. There is no intimation that the expedition imposed any penalty on Malcolm or in any way curtailed the territories he had annexed to his kingdom. And it may well be questioned whether the Dane, whose rule in England was so distinctly an interlude, could transmit any feudal right in Scotland to his successors. Certainly Denmark and Norway did not so pass, and claims to Scotland

---

[1] This date is questioned by both Robertson and Freeman, 1027–28 preferred.

[2] Early Kings, I, p. 97; II, p. 400. That the expression "he held that only a little while" does *not* refer to Malcolm's death is evident from the fact that the chroniclers use the phrase often, and always with reference to a rejection of allegiance. (A.-S. Chron., An. 947, 1091, etc.)

could only be made good in future by force of arms or new compacts.

Malcolm II, whom the Irish annalists entitle "Lord and Father of the West," had pushed his dominions southward to the Tweed. The line of Scoto-British princes in Strathclyde having failed with Eogan "the Bald," who fought with Malcolm at Carham, that province seems to have passed to the family of Malcolm, in the person of his son Duncan. Malcolm was able, whether by violence or otherwise, to set aside the prevailing custom and to secure the succession of Duncan as king of Scotland. With the death of Malcolm in 1034, the direct male line of Kenneth I became extinct. The succession should have passed to the line of Duff, had not the heir perished, probably by foul means, in 1033. This act left the rights of the crown to be transferred through the female line, by which the royal rights had been originally inherited, and occasioned a bloody strife between the families of Atholl and Moray, to which Duncan and Macbeth respectively belonged. The legitimate successor was Lulach, whose mother Macbeth married, thus becoming the guardian of Lulach during his minority. These claims had been set aside in favor of Malcolm's daughter's son, Duncan, who reigned from 1034 to 1040. He was opposed by Thorfin, son of a second daughter of Malcolm, who married one of the jarls of Orkney. The youthful Duncan was unsuccessful in his expedition against Thorfin, as he had also been in a foray into Northumberland, and was treacherously slain, "in the smith's bothy," near one of his unfortunate battlefields, by his rival Macbeth, who then seized the crown for himself.[1] Duncan left two sons, Malcolm Ceanmore and Donald Bane. Fordun is poor authority for the theory of a relationship between them and Siward, earl of Northumbria. Mr. Robertson says:

Malcolm II, 1005–1034 A. D.

Strathclyde Annexed

Break in Succession. Duncan, 1034– 1040 A. D.

Macbeth, 1040– 1058 A. D.

The flight of Duncan's children — mere infants — one to *Cumbria*,

[1] Sim. Dun., I, p. 90; Early Kings, I, p. 110; Norman Conq., II, p. 55.

the other to *the Isles*, is a fiction founded on the ideas of the time when it first appears, three or four centuries later. They probably remained amongst their hereditary partizans in Atholl and the southern provinces, occupying the same position which their cousin Lulach had done during the reign of their father—the position of the head of the Hy Nial, when Brian Boru achieved the sovereignty of Ireland; or of a Duke of Bavaria or Austria, in the olden time, when another magnate had been elected to the empire.[1]

This opinion is corroborated by the fact that Malcolm reigned till 1093 A. D., when he died in battle, apparently in the prime of manhood. He must, therefore, have been quite young in 1040, the date of his father's murder. Moreover, it would have been quite contrary to the custom of "fosterage," which prevailed among the Picts and Scots, for a member of the royal family to leave his own kinsmen and followers for an Anglo-Danish earl. By this custom

. . . . each 'full born' son having a claim upon the inheritance of his father . . . . was placed in the family of a dependant, who regarded such a charge as a mark of the highest confidence and honor; and even in the 17th century, men of rank and station in the Scottish Highlands still esteemed it a privilege to educate in this manner one of the children of the head of their lineage.[2]

In 1045 an attempt was made to vindicate the rights of Duncan's children, by their aged grandfather, the abbot of Dunkeld, which proved, however, premature. Nine years later Macbeth was attacked by Siward, earl of Northumbria, and put to flight. Two MSS. of the Chronicle record this event. No mention is made, however, of Malcolm or of Edward the Confessor, nor of the object of the expedition, but the facts that Macbeth *escaped* and that great booty was captured are explicitly noted. Of Macbeth's escape there can be no doubt.[3] He maintained himself in the kingdom till 1058, and after his

Is Defeated

**Malcolm III,
1058–1093 A. D.**

---

[1] Norman Conq., II, p. 55; Early Kings, I, p. 122, note.
[2] Early Kings, I, p. 34.
[3] A.-S. Chron., An. 1054 (Cott. Tiber., B. I; Cott. Tiber. B., IV); Norman Conq., II, p. 665; Early Kings, I, p. 122; Bain, I, p. xvii, note.

death his ward Lulach kept Malcolm from the throne several months longer. The Anglo-Norman writers consistently make this record a part of the chain of historical testimony whereby the feudal dependence of Scotland is maintained.

Feudal Influence Apparent in Chronicles

Fordun, in the same spirit, tries to maintain the side of the Scots. A good illustration of his authority is found in the statement that the Scots fled at the first sound of Malcolm's trumpet — a very different picture from the hard fight described by the English and Irish writers. Florence of Worcester writes:

Siward, the mighty Duke of Northumbria, by order of the King, entered Scotland with an army of cavalry and a strong fleet, and fought a battle with Macbeth King of the Scots; and many thousands of the Scots, and *all the Normans*, of whom mention was made above, being slain, he put him to flight, and established Malcolm, son of the King of the Cumbrians, as king, "ut rex jusserat."[1]

A careful study of this passage seems to justify the belief that Florence, compiling his account from several sources, is not entirely free from error. While he mentions the establishment of Malcolm as a reason for the expedition, the entire narrative implies that the Norman favorites of Edward who had taken refuge with Macbeth were the true cause of it.[2] He describes their expulsion from England, and apparently takes pains to call attention to them again in his account of the battle with Macbeth. The feeling of the English against them was intense. They had by their intrigues compelled Godwine to go into exile.[3] On his return the situation was reversed. But in 1054 Godwine had been dead upwards of a year, so that this expedition could not have been the result of his personal hostility toward his enemies. And of Harold Mr. Freeman says:

English Influence in Scotland

His policy of conciliation would forbid him to be needlessly harsh

[1] Ad. an. 1054.
[2] Sim. Dun. has no independent record of these events.
[3] Norman Conq., II, p. 125; Early Kings, II, p. 400.

even to a Norman, and he had every motive for dealing as tenderly as possible with all the wishes and prejudices of the King.

Hence there would be no reason for an order to issue from King Edward or Earl Harold which would devote the Normans to total destruction. Why should Edward attempt to aid a claimant to the Scottish throne at their expense? Macbeth had been ruling fourteen years. His reign was confessedly able and prosperous.[1] There is no indication of any feudal or hostile relation toward his southern neighbor. Why should Edward order the northern earl to attack him just at a time when the court favorites were finding refuge there? It would seem more reasonable that Siward acted on his own responsibility; that the flight of the Normans and the national hatred of them afforded an excellent pretext for an attempt to win back the ancient bounds of his earldom of Northumbria. If there was a relationship[2] between himself and Malcolm, it would furnish an additional reason for intervention on purely family grounds. In any event, Macbeth continued his reign till 1058, and as Siward died in 1055, it cannot be said that he established Malcolm as king. In general, it should be noted:

1. The extent to which the orders of the king had weight at this period, especially in the north, is very questionable. Royal writs during the reign of Edward the Confessor were very common in Wessex and East Anglia, but only one crossed the Humber, addressed to a Northumbrian earl, and that was in the days of Tostig.[3]

2. The jealousy which the great earls felt toward each other would render concerted action on their part unlikely.

3. Malcolm was not "regis Cumbrorum filium" at this time. His father Duncan was very likely placed over Strathclyde by Malcolm II. But Duncan had become *king of the Scots* twenty years before the invasion of 1054. The statement seems to be based on the erroneous belief, which the English chroniclers had,

---

[1] Norman Conq., II, pp. 55, 367, 369; Early Kings, I, p. 121.
[2] Celtic Scot, I, p. 408. Skene gives no authority for his statement.
[3] Norman Conq., II, p. 55.

that Macbeth directly succeeded Malcolm II in 1034, instead of Duncan in 1040, and is a clear evidence of the composite and in part unreliable nature of the record of Florence.[1]

4. Malcolm III (Ceanmore) became famous in English as well as Scottish history. He was, moreover, the first to receive a strictly feudal holding from an English king. Legend and romance had even in the days of Florence been busy with the names of Duncan, Macbeth, and Malcolm.[2] As Florence read his early English sources and compared them with this legendary material, it was easy to attribute to the weakness of Edward's reign the strength exhibited by the Conqueror, by William Rufus, and by Henry I. It was easy to infer that Siward's expedition, unaccounted for by the Chronicle, must have been by the order of the king, to unseat the usurper Macbeth and establish Malcolm, the vassal later of William the Conqueror—and therefore by inference of Edward the Confessor. But there is absolutely no evidence of homage paid by Scottish kings during the reign of Edward, nor of any feudal relation between the two kingdoms.[3]

With Florence of Worcester the feudalizing influence in the chronicles has only just begun to appear. There can be no doubt as to its purpose. It often discloses, and at the same time defeats its aim and end, by its gross exaggeration of truth, its perversions of known facts, or its open fraud and forgery. This throws doubt on the whole plea. Henry of Huntingdon relates how Siward sent his son into Scotland to conquer it. The son having met his death, the father advances into Scotland and, after defeating the king in battle, "*regnum totum destruxit, destructum sibi subjugavit*"! He is ignorant of any order of the king, and explains the invasion as one for the acquirement of territory. His extreme statement is entirely lacking in any historical basis. William of Malmesbury adds another element of

---

[1] Sim. Dun., Hist. Reg., II, p. 158.
[2] *Cf.* Shakespeare. It appears that "the meek and hoary" Duncan had not reached his prime. Siward also "was a hero whose history had a mythical element about it from the beginning." (Norman Conq., II, p. 374.)
[3] Florence is not above "an unsuccessful guess." (Norman Conq., IV, Note R.)

fiction in his statement that Macbeth was despoiled of *life* as well as of kingdom. Roger of Wendover gives the finishing touch:

Edwardus regnum Scotiae dedit Malcolmo, filio regis Cumbrorum, *de se tenendum*.[1]

Malcolm III and Tostig

After the death of Siward in 1035, Godwin's son Tostig received the earldom of Northumbria. Some sort of alliance or friendship seems to have existed between him and Malcolm. Simeon of Durham writes:

Interim rex Scottorum Malcolmus sui conjurati fratris, scilicet comitis Tostii, comitatum ferociter depopulatus est, violata pace Sancti Cuthberti in Lindisfarnensi insula.

This was in 1061,

.... Edwardo regnante, quando Tosti comes Eboracensis profectus Romam fuerat.

Of this "sworn brotherhood" Mr. Freeman says, "This was a tie by which reconciled enemies often sought to bind one another to special friendship."[2] He considers that the tie must have been formed some time between 1055 and 1061. It seems most reasonable to infer that it was soon after Malcolm's accession to the crown in 1058; also that it was sought by Tostig rather than Malcolm, who was now secure in his rights. It is only thus that Malcolm's raid over the border, for which Tostig in no way inflicted any retribution, can be explained.

The hour of the conquest is at hand. Invaluable as the works of the monastic chroniclers are to the historian, it is a relief to turn from their oft-conflicting tales to the more trustworthy records of the feudal era which now dawns in its fullness upon England.

---

[1] Hen. Hunt., p. 194; W. Malmes., Ad. an.; Flor., Hist., I, p. 573. Roger died 1237 A.D.

[2] Sim. Dun., Hist. Reg., II, pp. 174, 221; Norman Conq., II, p. 392.

CHAPTER III.

THE INFLUENCE OF THE NORMAN KINGS IN SCOTLAND.

The reign of the Normans in England marks the establishment of a definite feudal policy, consistently followed by the kings of England and Scotland till the days of Edward I. Its rapid and marvelous development was radically affected by the allied policy of intermarriage between the royal houses of the two realms, hitherto strongly antagonistic.

Beginning of a Definite Feudal Policy

The court of the king of Scots, like that of Flanders or Denmark, had often proved a refuge for those compelled by the chance of war or by political intrigue to flee from England. In the summer of 1068 A. D.[1] such a band of exiles, having aroused the suspicion of William the Conqueror, or fearing his wrath, had sought refuge with Malcolm III, in the land of the Scots. With Merlesweyne, Cospatric, and other influential leaders of the English party, came Edgar Atheling, attended by his mother and two sisters, Christina and Margaret. The Princess Margaret speedily won the heart of the Scottish king, and the union of the lines of Cerdic and McAlpin gave to the Scots their first claim to the English crown. It was an event of the greatest moment, not only because of its immediate effect on the welfare of Scotland, but also because of the far-reaching influences which take their source from it. Editha, a daughter of this royal pair, became the wife of Henry I of England. Three sons, Edgar, Alexander, and David, destined to attain the kingship and to control the national policy, grew up under their care, acquiring daily from their mother English sympathies and tastes. It will not be

Influenced by Inter-Marriage

---

[1] Fl. Wig.; Sim. Dun., Hist. Reg., An. 1068. On date cf. Early Kings, I, p. 130, note.

strange, therefore, under this bond of blood-relationship, to find heirs to the Scottish crown maintaining intimate relations with their kinsfolk at the English court. But even under the great Edward, when the drift of the nobility was almost wholly in favor of submission to his suzerainty, the Scots themselves, as a people, constantly preserve their spirit of independence, their purpose to acknowledge no foreign overlordship in the affairs of their kingdom.

The marriage of Margaret and Malcolm bound the king of Scots to his brother-in-law, Edgar Atheling, identifying him with the efforts of the English to throw off the Conqueror's yoke, and restore their native dynasty. But apparently he did not directly co-operate in the combined attack of Danes and English upon York (1069). Nor did William extend his ravages beyond the Tyne.[1] On the return of the Conqueror to the south, however, Malcolm crossed the border.

Malcolm Invades England
Holding Cumberland by right of conquest,[2] he passed through it, and then, turning eastward as already noted, ravaged the valley of the Tees to the coast. Cospatric, who but a short time before had found shelter and welcome at the Scottish court, had made his peace again with William, and had bought a title to the earldom of Northumberland. Forgetting Malcolm's kindness, he now invaded Cumberland, carried off large booty, and shut himself up in the castle of Bamborough. Malcolm's revenge was second only to the terrible punishment which the Conqueror inflicted on the north. The chronicler of Durham dilates on the atrocities committed, and declares that "even to this day" not a hovel can be found in Scotia without slaves of English blood.[3] It is a little strange that the English overlord (?) should have allowed his vassal to take such liberties with English subjects, and that a restoration of the captives

---

[1] A.-S. Chron.; Sim. Dun., Hist. Reg., An. 1069.

[2] Sim. Dun., Hist. Reg., II, p. 191. Erat enim eo tempore Cumbreland sub regis Malcolmi dominio, non jure possessa sed violenter subjugata.

[3] Sim. Dun., Hist. Reg., II., pp. 190–2.

should not have been required. The invasion was, however, not forgotten, and in 1072 A. D. William set out for Scotland — not to punish a rebellious vassal or require a restoration of captives, but to secure his northern border against attack by a foreign foe. It is unlikely that the English exiles were here at this time, though they may have fled on William's approach, as Edgar returned from Flanders to Scotland in 1074.[1] The record of the meeting between Malcolm and William is brief :

Meeting of William and Malcolm III, 1072

In this year King William led a naval force and a land force to Scotland, and lay about that land with ships on the sea side ; and himself with his land-force went in over the ford, and he there found naught for which they were the better.[2] And King Malcolm came and made peace with King William, and gave hostages and was his man ; and the king went home with all his force.[3]

The brief record gives no clue as to that for which Malcolm became the man of the Conqueror. Later events, however, throw some light on the question.

In 1079 Malcolm came into England "with a large force, and harried Northumberland until he came to the Tyne, and slew many hundred men; and led home many treasures, and precious things, and men in captivity."[4] As William was fighting with his son Robert in Normandy, this raid may have been prompted by Malcolm's friendship for the duke, or simply by a desire for plunder. It illustrates how lightly the feudal oath rested on men's consciences in these days — Malcolm was no exception — and how little real significance it had for the king of Scots and his people. In 1080 William and Robert were reconciled to each other, and the duke was sent against Malcolm. But the

Subsequent Invasions of England

---

[1] A.-S. Chron., An. 1075.

[2] Possibly referring to the escape of Edgar and his English followers. The crossing was probably at the fords of the Forth, fortified by Kenneth II in the days of Edgar. Fl. Wig. says the meeting was " in loco qui dicitur Abernitbici."

[3] A.-S. Chron., An. 1073.

[4] A.-S. Chron., Fl. Wig., Ad. an.

expedition was a failure.¹ Sir Francis Palgrave tries to prove that such an expedition occurred in 1068-9. He says that Malcolm refused obedience to William the Conqueror, who then sent Robert to enforce it. The military tenants were summoned, among whom was Adelelm, abbot of Abingdon. Robert was instructed to offer peace to the Scots in case of obedience, otherwise war. Malcolm met the English forces in Lothian, and acknowledged that the dominion of Scotland was subject to the crown of England. The story is based on the Book of Abingdon (compiled not earlier than the reign of Henry III).²

"This important transaction," says Palgrave, "which is related with great obscurity by Orderic Vitalis (p. 511), is told clearly and distinctly in the book of Abingdon. In consequence of the abbot being personally present, the compiler of that most authentic and valuable volume was, without doubt, better acquainted with the circumstances than other writers could be, who had not the same sources of information."³ The obscure passage from Orderic, which Palgrave tries to elucidate with the Book of Abingdon, is as follows:

The bishop of Durham [Aegelwina], also, being reconciled to King William, became the mediator for peace with the king of the Scots, and was the bearer into Scotland of the terms offered by William. Though the aid of Malcolm had been solicited by the English, and he had prepared to come to their succor with a strong force, yet when he heard what the envoy had to propose with respect to a peace, he remained quiet, and joyfully sent back ambassadors in company with the bishop of Durham, who in his name swore fealty to King William. In thus preferring peace to war, he best consulted his own welfare, and the inclination of his subjects; for the people of Scotland, though fierce in war, love ease and quiet, and are not disposed to disturb themselves

---

¹ Sim. Dun., Hist. Reg., An. 1080.

"It seems certain Robert reaped no special glory in his Scottish expedition." No authority for the legend that Malcolm met Robert in Lothian and gave hostages. (Norman Conq., IV, p. 671.) "Whether from want of conduct on the part of the commander or of efficiency in the troops, the expedition was shamefully unsuccessful." (Palgrave, England and Normandy, III, p. 548.)

² Early Kings, II, Note Q.

³ Palgrave, Eng. Com., II, p. cccxxxi.

about their neighbors' affairs, loving rather religious exercises than those of arms.[1]

Now the citation from the Book of Abingdon is clearly proved to have been transferred from the year 1080, where it belongs.[2] The true nature of the expedition of 1080, and hence of the supposed expedition of 1068–9, has already been explained, and characterized as "shamefully unsuccessful." The passage from Orderic, therefore, remains as "obscure" as ever, and the impression is confirmed that it is nothing more than "a confused and erroneous version of the events which actually took place in 1072, transferred by one of his usual blunders to 1068."[3] A careful examination of the work of Orderic, however great its value in other respects, makes it impossible to accept his testimony in regard to Scottish history as a safe basis for argument. He was born in 1075. At the age of ten he was sent to Normandy, and spent the remainder of his days in the monastery of St. Evroult. He probably visited England once, possibly twice, for a few weeks, but no more. It would not be strange, therefore, to find his work representing the gossip and hearsay of the times, or his own imaginings, rather than the facts of history. All the passages relating to Scotland exemplify this. That on the submission of 1868–9 is unique. *Not another chronicler* was aware of any such event. It contradicts the facts of history in its characterization of the Scots—a contradiction which Palgrave endorses, when he says: "A strong desire for religious contemplation and domestic tranquillity existed among the Gael of Albania. Malcolm's determination of submitting to William was received by the clans with the greatest joy—as a boon, and not an humiliation. His embassadors, accompanied by the Bishop of Durham, appeared before the Conqueror, and the oath of fealty, taken by proxy, renewed the bond of dependence between

[1] Ord. Vit., II, p. 19.
[2] Robertson, Early Kings, II, Ap. Q; Freeman, Norm. Conq., IV, Note X.
[3] "Edgar and his partizans passed the whole of the following winter in Scotland, which the Conqueror would surely have provided against had he already received the submission of Malcolm." Orderic "*alone* passes over without notice the really important meeting between the two kings in 1072." (Early Kings, II, Ap. Q.)

the kings of the Scots and the Basileus of the British Islands."[1] Yet it was under Malcolm III that five of the most cruel Scottish raids known were made into English territory, and on his death these Gael who were so desirous for "religious contemplation" began a fight to expel the English whom Malcolm had brought into Scotland—a fight which ended in the death of the claimant to the throne who had English support. Orderic describes at length the expedition of William Rufus, in 1092, against Malcolm, recounts the conversations which took place back and forth between the two kings on the impassable banks of the Forth, and the negotiations with Count Robert. He makes Malcolm confess that King Edward had given him the county of Lothian with the hand of his niece Margaret—a fact quite unknown to other chroniclers. The negotiations for peace are finally concluded. The two armies are disbanded, and the two kings depart for England together. Malcolm, wishing after a time to return to Scotland, is murdered on the way by Robert de Mowbray. "The King of England and his great nobles hearing of this, were deeply distressed, being ashamed that so foul and cruel a deed should be done by Normans."[2] Such sentiments were truly characteristic of William Rufus! Edgar then succeeded Malcolm, but, being opposed by Donald, was slain. Alexander then slew Donald and ascended the throne. This, as will soon appear, directly contradicts well-known facts. Orderic, therefore, as an *original* authority on Scotland, may hereafter be left undisturbed in his monastic seclusion.

It seems probable that there was some tie of friendship between Malcolm III and Robert, the eldest son of the Conqueror. Instances of playing into each other's hands have already been noted. It is Robert and Edgar Atheling who

---

[1] Mr. Freeman says, however (1068), "Scotland Bernicia, and the northwestern shires of Mercia, were still left in their precarious independence." And again, "The men of the still independent England beyond the Tees." (Norman Conq., IV, pp. 207, 254.)

[2] Ord. Vit., Eccl. Hist., III, p. 11.

negotiate the final treaty between Malcolm and William Rufus;
and apparently William's failure to keep his engage-
Agreement between Malcolm and William ments occasioned the departure, about Christmas time, 1091, of both Robert and Edgar from the English court.¹ In its account of these transactions the Chronicle gives the first definite intimation of the feudal arrangements between Malcolm and William the Conqueror.

While King William was out of England, King Malcolm of Scotland came hither into England, and harried a great deal of it, until the good men who had charge of this land sent a force against him, and turned him back. When King William of Normandy heard of this, he made ready for his departure, and came to England, and his brother the count Robert with him, and forthwith ordered a force to be called out, both a ship-force and a land-force; but the ship-force, ere he could come to Scotland, almost all perished miserably; .... and the king and his brother went with the land-force. But when King Malcolm heard that they would seek him with a force, he went with his force out of Scotland into the district of Leeds (provincia Loidis, Fl. Wigorn.) in England and there awaited. When King William with his force approached, then intervened Count Robert and Eadgar aetheling, and so made a reconciliation between the Kings; so that King William came to our King, and became his man, with all such obedience as he had before paid to his father, and that with oath confirmed. And King William promised him in land and in all things that which he had had before under his father.²

Florence of Worcester says that besides the destruction of William's fleet many of his horsemen also perished with cold and hunger before he could reach Scotland. Malcolm came to meet him with an army "in provincia Loidis." Earl Robert, perceiving this, concluded a peace between the two kings, with the assistance of Edgar Atheling, "ea conditione, ut Willelmo, sicut patri suo obedivit, Malcolmus obediret; et Malcolmo xii. villas, quas in Anglia sub patre illius habuerat, Willelmus redderet, et xii. marcas auri singulis annis daret."³ Simeon adds the infor-

¹ A.-S. Chron., An. 1091; Early Kings, I, p. 142.
² A.-S. Chron., An. 1091.   ³ Fl. Wig., II, p. 29.

mation that William came to Durham and restored the bishop to his seat. He continues, "Sed antequam rex intrasset Scotiam"— and from this point quotes from the chronicle of Worcester concerning the destruction of the English forces. Malmesbury passes his judgment on the expedition in the words "nihil magnificentia sua dignum exhibuit; militibus desideratis, jumentis interceptis." Roger of Wendover illustrates the spirit in which the later writers approach such events when he says that Malcolm, "*nimio terrore percussus*," did homage to William and swore fealty.[1]

A comparison of these materials makes certain points clear:

1. Malcolm *sought* a meeting with William.
2. The destruction of a large part of William's forces left him in no position to *compel* Malcolm to an agreement.
3. The agreement negotiated between the two kings had for its basis the treaty to which Malcolm and the Conqueror were parties in 1072. Malcolm was to render the same obedience to William that he had rendered to his father, and William was to restore to Malcolm the twelve manors he had "*in Anglia*" under the Conqueror, and to pay him twelve marks of gold each year.

Such an agreement was quite in accord with the keen-sighted policy of the great William. He had won England. But how to keep it was not an easy problem. It does not seem that his thoughts extended beyond the consolidation of England and Normandy. If they did, there were richer lands to conquer than the barren north. He treated the Scots very much as he did the Danes, buying their inactivity or peace, that he might, by thus securing his borders, develop the internal strength and unity of his kingdom. Any other policy would have been almost suicidal, even for the Conqueror. Some such arrangement with the Scots as had been made with the Danes during the revolt of the north might, therefore, be reasonably expected. It took the form of an annual pension or subsidy in gold, together with certain lands in England, for which Malcolm did homage.[2] It

---

[1] Hist. Reg., II, p. 218; Gesta Reg. Ang., II, p. 365; Flor. Hist., An. 1090.

[2] A somewhat similar policy was followed in the pacification of the Highlands in 1691–2. (Gardiner, Student's Hist. Eng., p. 653.)

is hardly conceivable that Malcolm would surrender without a blow the independence of his kingdom, or that William Rufus would consider his suzerainty *over Scotland* dearly bought, at such a price. Yet William was certainly unwilling to comply with his treaty obligations, while Malcolm was equally anxious to have them fulfilled — an attitude on the part of both kings that indicates that Malcolm's homage was for this grant of the Conqueror in England. Mr. Freeman, seeking with his wonted persistency and ingenuity to establish his theory of Lothian as an English earldom, says: "At this stage Lothian was the land held within the Kingdom of England; it was what Northumberland, Huntingdon, or any other confessedly English land held by the Scottish King, was in later times." For this statement he cites no authority. Again he says: "One would like to know whether the 'xii. villae quas in Anglia sub patre illius [Willelmi Rufi sc.] habuerat [Malcolmus]' were in Lothian or where." Mr. Round, whose critical research has exposed many of the fallacious theories propounded by Mr. Freeman and others, has incidentally given at least a partial answer to this query in his discussion of the Northamptonshire Geld-Roll. "Although written in old English, it is well subsequent to the conquest," but "cannot be later than 1075. . . . . Of the very few names mentioned, one may surprise and the other puzzle us. The former is that of 'the Scot King,' holding land even then in a shire where his successors were to hold it so largely." This reference, taken with two such sources as the Chronicle and Florence of Worcester, is certainly significant, nor does it require any stretch of imagination to conclude that these Northamptonshire lands were connected with the Conqueror's grant to Malcolm III. Unfortunately the reference is not definite enough to do more than suggest the fact of such holdings by the Scot king. It may also be urged that this document proves too much, that possibly these lands were held prior to the grant of the Conqueror — thereby implying homage and a closer relation than has been admitted hitherto. But conceding, at most, that Malcolm Ceanmore was related to Siward, that he lived in England in exile during the reign of Macbeth, perhaps here in Northamptonshire, and that the earl of Northumberland, with the consent, if not at the command, of Edward the Confessor, aided him in his first attempts to regain his kingdom, the admission does not touch the main point at issue, viz., the independence of the kingdom of Scotland. For it is inconceivable that the weak Confessor King should have enjoyed — apparently without lifting a finger — or that his powerful successors should have lost, what Henry II wrung by special charters from the dire necessity of his royal captive, William the Lion, and what the great Edward appropriated, only after the failure of all direct heirs to the Scottish crown left the kingdom to be the spoil of anarchy. The truer view and the one most in accord with the best sources, is that the Scottish kings did not hold definite feudal fiefs in England till this grant of the Conqueror.[1]

Two years passed, and then

.... the King of Scotland sent and demanded the fulfilment of the treaty that had been promised him. And King William summoned him to Gloucester, and sent him hostages to Scotland, and Eadgar aetheling afterwards, and the men back again, who brought him with great worship to the king. But when he came to the king, he could not be held worthy the speech of our king, or the conditions that had been previously promised him, and therefore in great hostility they parted, and King Malcolm returned home to Scotland. But as soon as he came home, he gathered his army, and marched into England, harrying with more animosity than ever behoved him. And then Robert, the earl of Northumberland, ensnared him with his men unawares, and slew him. With him also was slain his son Edward, who should, if he had lived, have been king after him.[2]

Malcolm's action may have been prompted by William's

---

[1] Norman Conq., I, Note I; Wm. Rufus, I, p. 303; Round, Feudal Eng., pp. 147–8. I am greatly indebted to Mr. Round for the favor of a personal letter, giving the results of a special examination of the puzzling passage in the Northampt. Geld-Roll, and of others which might have a bearing on it. But neither he nor Mr. W. H. Stevenson (probably the best authority on eleventh century Anglo-Saxon) has been able to determine, as yet, its exact meaning and force. Mr. Round takes it to imply ownership at the time. Mr. Stevenson thinks the entry may be corrupt.

[2] A.-S. Chron., An. 1093.

invasion of Cumberland, in which he drove out Dolphin, the son of Cospatric, seizing and fortifying Carlisle. By a grant to Cospatric, after his flight from England, he and his descendants became vassals of the king of Scots, and Dolphin probably held in Cumberland under Malcolm, who might well object to the high-handed policy of William Rufus. Hence the demand for a fulfilment of the treaty of 1091. William had fallen so seriously ill at Gloucester "that he was everywhere reported dead.' His weakness made him more willing to listen to the appeals of his primates that a firm peace should be established with Scotland.[1] But returning health revived his arrogance, and he refused to meet Malcolm, hoping to compel him to "do right" in his own court, and in the presence of English barons only. But Malcolm indignantly refused to do right "nisi in regnorum suorum confiniis, ubi reges Scottorum erant soliti rectitudinem facere regibus Anglorum, et secundum judicium primatum utriusque regni." Returning to his own land, he prepared for the war in which he lost his life.[2]

The words which the chronicler puts in the mouth of Malcolm show what the custom was in the later age in which he wrote, after the feudal relation had been definitely established for several generations. Mr. Robertson says:

> Certain inferences are sometimes drawn from the expression *rectitudinem facere*, 'to do right,'—though it is always dangerous to lay too much stress upon the strict and exact *legal* meaning of every word employed by a chronicler,—and it is implied that 'right' could only be 'done' by 'a vassal to his superior,' and that therefore Malcolm was William's vassal—*for the Kingdom of Scotland.* The simple answer to this is, that not an acre of land could be held under the feudal system by 'noble tenure' except by homage, or vassalage, the extent of the vassalage being identical with the extent of the fief, and not necessarily implying the entire dependance of the holder upon the overlord of the fief. He might hold *other fiefs* of innumerable other over-

---

[1] Norman Conq., V, p. 118; Sim. Dun., II, pp. 196-9; A.-S. Chron., An. 1092-3; Skene, Celtic Scot., I, p. 430.

[2] Fl. Wig., Sim. Dun., Hist. Reg., An. 1093; on Wm. Malmes., Gest. Reg. Ang., II, p. 366, *cf.* Early Kings, I, p. 145, note.

lords. Thus in a treaty of peace between Philip Augustus and Richard, the latter agrees 'ut ipse faciet Regi Franciae *servitia et justicias in curia Regis Franciae* de singulis feodis quos ab eo tenet' (Foed., Vol. I, Pt. I, p. 61), ... without in the least implying the subjection of the English crown to the French. *Rectitudo* simply means 'a right,' and when Prince Alexander performed homage to John 'pro omnibus *rectitudinibus*, etc.,' and when Richard, by his Charter of Privileges, confirmed to William 'omnes libertates et *rectitudines*, etc.,' the 'rights' were claimed of the English crown, and in the latter case settled 'secundum quod recognoscetur a quatuor proceribus nostris . . . . et a quatuor proceribus illius,' exactly as Malcolm claimed on this occasion . . . . If a question was to be raised about the right, it was to be decided not 'secundum judicium tantum baronum . . . . in curia [Willielmi]' but 'secundum judicium primatum *utriusque* regni' and on the frontiers (Doc. Illust. Hist. Scot., XV, sec. 19; Foed., Vol. I, Pt. I, pp. 50–62).[1]

There seems no doubt, therefore, that Malcolm's relation to the Conqueror and to his son was that of a holder of certain lands in England—for which, and for an annual subsidy of gold, he did homage. That he did not stand in a feudal relation to William for Lothian might be inferred from the fact that he granted, without remonstrance from the Conqueror, Dunbar, and the adjacent lands in Lothian, to Cospatric, after he had rebelled against the Norman king. It indicates that William's policy was to secure peace on the border rather than overlordship in Lothian.[2]

The unexpected death of Malcolm's son and successor, Edward, threw the kingdom into great confusion, and made English interference possible. The conditions were similar in many respects to those which prevailed in England after the death of Henry I. How strong was the opposition to the English became apparent in the broils and tumults which followed Malcolm's death. The Chronicle reads:

Disorder follows Malcolm's Death

The Scots then chose Donald, Malcolm's brother, for king, and

[1] Early Kings, I, pp. 144–5; II, p. 402, notes.
[2] On Malcolm's character *cf.* Early Kings, *in loco*, and Celtic Scot., I, p. 432.

drove out all the English who were before with King Malcolm. When Duncan, King Malcolm's son, who was in King William's court,—his father having before given him as a hostage to our king's father, and he had so remained afterwards,—heard all that had thus taken place, he came to the king, and performed such fealty as the king would have of him, and so, with his permission went to Scotland, with the support that he could get of English and French, and deprived his kinsman Donald of the kingdom, and was received for king.[1] But some of the Scots afterwards gathered together, and slew almost all his followers, and he himself with a few escaped. Afterwards they were reconciled, on the condition that he never again should harbor in the land either English or French.

This illustrates anew the steady opposition of the native Scots to English intervention in their affairs. The following year Duncan was killed and Donald restored. He reigned for three years, and was then driven out by Edgar Atheling, who came with an English army to establish his namesake, the son of the English Margaret and Malcolm, as king of the Scots.[2] It cannot be doubted that Edgar, like Duncan, sustained some feudal relation to the king of England, but what it was can only be learned incidentally from the later history. As it is not referred to as a special precedent, or basis of comparison, as in the case of Malcolm IV, it could hardly have been more than an indefinite and temporary relation, fitting in naturally with the troubled condition of the times and the kinship which existed between the royal families.

Before passing to the reign of Henry I, two points require notice.

1. The meeting place of Malcolm and William Rufus. If it was in Lothian, what is meant by this designation? In general Lothian is regarded as part or all of the region lying between the Forth and the Tweed. But what was its relation to Bernicia, Saxonia, Northumbria? The Roman restrained the incursions of the Picts by a wall from Tynemouth to Solway, and it seems that the Scots at times laid

Meeting Place of 1091

---

[1] The Scots were evidently taken by surprise. (A.-S. Chron., An. 1093-4.)
[2] A.-S. Chron., 1094.

claim to the district north of this line as theirs by right of inheritance. Northumbria had a varying boundary, and the region from Tyne to Forth seems to have been included, now under the name Bernicia, again under Saxonia, and sometimes under the varying names of Lothian. "The Border" was an exceedingly unstable quantity. But in the feudal period Lothian seems to have been always shut off from the Tweed by the Scotish March. The similarity, in the Latin, of Lothian and Leeds has increased the confusion. Beda twice refers to Loidis, and it seems pretty clear that to his mind "regio Loidis" meant the district of Leeds.[1]

The A.-S. Chronicle reads, "when King Malcolm heard that they [William and Robert] would seek him with a force, he went with his force *ut of Scotlande into Lothene on Englaland* and there awaited" (1091). This Mr. Thorpe translates "the district of Leeds," in accordance with Florence of Worcester, who wrote "provincia Loidis." It should be remembered that Florence followed a copy of the Chronicle which has not been preserved. Simeon of Durham and later writers agree with Florence in using "provincia Loidis," though in 1018 Simeon designates *Lothian* as "Lodoneium." Walter of Hemingburgh writes "provincia Lowdicensis juxta confinia ad resistendum praeparatus."[2]

Was the meeting of Malcolm and William, then, in the district of Leeds, or north of the Tweed in what was definitely known as Lothian, or at some place between the Tyne and Tweed, in the region anciently claimed by the Picts and Scots? Mr. Burton maintains the first view, and is supported by Mr. Thorpe's translation of the Chronicle.[3] Mr. Skene and English writers oppose this view in favor of the second.[4] Pinkerton is a strong advocate of the third view, making the place of meeting in the modern county of Northumberland.[5]

There is at least one objection to a meeting in the district of

[1] Beda, Bk. II, Cap. 14; Bk. III, Cap. 24; Celtic Scot., I, p. 254.
[2] Chronicon, I, p. 23.   [4] Celtic Scot., I, p. 429, note.
[3] Hist. Scot., I, pp. 378, 444, notes.
[5] An Enquiry, etc., II, p. 209. *Cf.* Hailes' Annals, I, p. 24.

Leeds. It may be inferred from Simeon's narrative that William advanced as far north as Durham, and restored the bishop to his see, before the loss of his forces prevented his entrance into Scotland. Hence a meeting with Malcolm in the district of Leeds could only be brought about by a retreat on William's part to the south. There is no positive evidence to prove such a retreat, but there is nothing against it. William was in a region which had always been a menace to English kings. Here, "the authority of the king and the unity of the monarchy were most likely to be threatened." Malcolm had completed the Conqueror's work of desolation in the land, so that its own inhabitants had to flee to escape starvation. William had reached Durham, but in the unseasonable period which he chose the expedition had met with serious disaster, by sea and land. He might well hesitate about entering a hostile country with a starving army and no supplies, to meet a formidable enemy who had his kingdom at his back. Is it unreasonable to suppose, therefore, that after the disaster to his fleet and army William fell back on the province of Leeds, whither Malcolm, anxious for a renewal of the grant of the Conqueror, came and awaited either an attack or negotiations for peace? Mr. Haddan, in discussing the church of Cumbria, marks the northern boundary of the district of Leeds, and it appears that if William had retreated south and west only across the Tees, Florence and Simeon might naturally, and with propriety, have spoken of him as being "in provincia Loidis." It is noticeable, also, that on the return journey Florence does not speak of William as going *from Lothian through* Northumbria, as might have been expected, had he been north of the Tweed, but *from Northumbria through Mercia*.[1] As evidence that this meeting occurred north of Durham (and therefore in Lothian!), Mr. Freeman cites a "Carta Willielmi Dunelmensis Episcopi de ecclesiis Alverton Siggestune at Brunton," which is witnessed, among others, by the king and his brothers Robert and Henry, as also by Duncan (son of Malcolm III

[1] Norman Conq., IV, p. 349; Haddan and Stubbs, Counc., II, Pt. I, pp. 10-11; Fl. Wig., II, p. 29.

by Ingebiorg) and Edgar Atheling. As Edgar had been expelled from his lands in Normandy and had fled to Scotland, he could not have signed such a charter till after the reconciliation between Malcolm and William, which included the renewal of friendly relations between William and himself. And as both Robert and Edgar Atheling withdrew from the English court just before Christmas of 1091, the charter could not have been signed after that time. Mr. Freeman infers, therefore, that it must have been witnessed sometime between the last of September and the Christmas *gemot*—probably at Durham, on the southward march from Scotland. Hence William must have advanced into Lothian! The argument is ingenious, but it rests on a very unsubstantial basis. The charter itself is of a very dubious character. It is found in bad company. The charters which precede and follow it are clearly fraudulent. And even this one, as Mr. Freeman admits, has some startling elements which make its authenticity doubtful. It has been considered that Henry was not in England at this time. Malmesbury is the sole authority for the contrary view, and is opposed by Orderic, whom both Freeman and Palgrave so frequently rely on to prop up their theories of an English Imperium and its Scottish dependency. Furthermore, granting the genuineness of the charter, there is not the slightest ground for saying that it was witnessed at Durham, on the southward march from Lothian. Rather, there is much against such a view. There were nearly three months after the treaty with Malcolm was completed, and before the departure of Edgar and Robert from the English Court, in which the Durham charter might have been witnessed. Among the names appended are those of the archbishop of York, the bishops of Lincoln, Bath, and Salisbury, the abbots of St. Augustine, St. Edmunds, and St. Mary, Robert the Chancellor, and " Ranulphi thessarii,' besides presbyters, earls, and others. It is almost inconceivable that Simeon, the Durham chronicler, should have specially, and in detail, noted the visit of William to Durham, and the restoration of the bishop to his see, only to pass over in absolute silence such a gathering of prominent clerics and laics, and so important an event as the confirmation by the Red King of a charter to Durham. The prevalence of forged charters at Durham, and the "singular and startling" character of this one, forbid its use as evidence that William Rufus advanced beyond the Scottish border in the expedition of 1091.[1]

A meeting place in the border country, south of the Tweed, has more in its favor. There is no doubt that Malcolm went out of Scotland into England to meet William. Now, if Lothian was a part of Scotland at this time, the meeting could not have occurred there. If, on the other hand, it was English, as Freeman and Palgrave claim, the statement of the chronicler that Malcolm went out of Scotland "into Lothene on Englaland" is quite without point. He would never think of saying the king went from Gloucester to Hereford in England, unless there were a Hereford in Wales, which he wished to distinguish. That is to say, a Lothian in England implies clearly a Lothian in Scotland, which could be nothing else than part or all of the region between the Forth and Tweed. And if plain Lothian did not mean the region north of the Tweed, surely "Lothene on Englaland" would not make such a meaning any more clear. Indulf had made the first step toward its acquirement by seizing Edinburgh stronghold (952). After the battle of Carham Eadulf Cudel ceded the whole district, which may have extended south of the Tweed, to the king of the Scots. Thereafter it remained in his hands. The Scots, through the Picts, had a claim to all the northern portion of Bernicia, from the Tyne to the Forth. The unsettled condition of the border, which continued till a much later period, favored the extension of Scottish dominion over this district, because of its contiguity to the seat of Scottish power. The author of the article on Lothian in the Britannica says: "There is no trace of any special homage for Lothian except in two dubious charters by Edgar to William Rufus, so that it seems certain that from the beginning of the 11th Century it was an integral part of Scotland. Freeman, in his Historical

---

[1] Freeman, Wm. Rufus, I, pp. 296–307; II, note P; Hist. Dun. Script. Tres. (Raine), Ap. XXII.

Geography, styles it an English earldom, but it is never so called in any authentic record."

The conclusion seems inevitable. The meeting must have been in the district of Leeds, or in the border marches south of the Tweed. The latter location is confirmed by another citation from the Chronicle, which, in 1125, mentions the fact that J., bishop of Lothene, went to Rome. Mr. Haddan shows that this refers to John, bishop of Glasgow, who was consecrated by Paschal II about 1117, and died in 1147. His see varied in its bounds, and in the jurisdiction to which it was subject. Scottish *kings* ruled over Cumberland and Westmoreland, as well as Scottish Cumbria, from 1070 to 1091, but Glasgow *bishops*, from 1053 to 1114, were probably consecrated at York. Conflicting claims arose as to jurisdiction. Durham claimed Teviotdale, while York claimed Glasgow. About 1100 English Cumbria and Teviotdale were taken from Durham, the former being assigned to York, the latter to Glasgow. "Glasgow is found in possession of Teviotdale, and indeed of all Roxburghshire south of the Tweed, at the revival of that See by David, A. D. 1107–1124, thus bringing down Durham to nearly its later northern boundary. And Glasgow, of course, also *claimed* Cumbria."[1] The see of Glasgow, therefore, or the bishopric of Lothene, had as its southern boundary pretty much the present line of demarcation between Scotland and England, but did not embrace the region known as the Scottish March and Lothian proper. When Lothian was ceded to Malcolm II in 1018, its ecclesiastical jurisdiction was transferred from Durham to the Scottish bishop. But it "did not at any time include Teviotdale, which remained subject to Durham until about A. D. 1100, and was then seized by Glasgow." Hence Teviotdale at this time, though politically allied with, if not subject to Scotland, was ecclesiastically under the see of Durham or Glasgow, and might have been regarded by the monastic chronicler, together with the whole of Roxburghshire south of the Tweed, as the English portion of the bishopric of Lothene, or Glas-

[1] H. and S., Counc., Vol. II, Pt. I, pp. 10–13, 16, 23.

gow.[1] This region would afford an advantageous position in which Malcolm could await William Rufus, and is the very situation chosen nearly a century later by William the Lion in his dealings with John. A study of the sources from this standpoint strengthens the conviction that the meeting was not in the region generally known as Lothian.

2. The influences set in motion by Queen Margaret, making the connection between the Scottish and English churches closer, were continued by her sons. Though they operated mainly in the realm of the church, they reached out into the political and territorial relations of the two kingdoms. Christianity gained access to south Britain at a very early date, through Roman channels, and to the north in the fifth and sixth centuries, chiefly through Irish missionaries. Augustine was commissioned to go to Britain A. D. 597, and was consecrated after his arrival by the archbishop of Arles, with the pope's consent. He was to consecrate, *per singula loca*, twelve bishops subject to himself, and after his death to a metropolitan at London. He was also to consecrate a bishop of York, who in turn, having received his *pallium* from the pope, should consecrate twelve others subordinate to himself. After the death of Augustine the two sees were to be equal in principle, precedence being given to the occupant of the see of first origin. Difficulties arose which prevented the realization of this scheme, chief among which was the independent spirit of the Scots in regard to their church relations. Their ecclesiastical capital was Dunkeld, under Kenneth MacAlpin, but about 907 A. D. the seat of the head bishop was removed to St. Andrews. His position was that of a diocesan bishop, of whom there were few in Scotland till the twelfth century.[2] Conflict between York and Canterbury as to jurisdiction arose very soon. Councils were held in 1072 at Winchester and Windsor, in which the Humber was recognized as the boundary between

[marginal note: Queen Margaret and the Church]

---

[1] Haddan and Stubbs, Counc., Vol. II, Pt. I, p. 142, note. For map, see Celtic Scot. *Cf.* Pinkerton, An Enquiry, etc., Vol. II, p. 209.

[2] Makower, Const. Hist., Ch. Eng., p. 105.

the two sees. Scotland was without doubt intended to form part of the northern diocese, as Wales did of the southern. But "political causes kept the Northumbrian primate from exercising any effective authority north of the Tweed and Solway. . . . . Scotland was never subdued to any practical purpose, and the result was that the archbishops of York were left with a vast region under their diocesan care, and with the single suffragan see of Durham under their metropolitan jurisdiction." The popes at first ratified the Scottish subjection to York, but the Scot kings, mainly on national grounds, refused their assent to any such transference of rights, while the Scottish clergy made a lasting resistance to the pretensions of York. In 1188 A. D., under William the Lion, their claims were conceded, and Clement III declared the Scottish bishops immediately subject to the papal see. In 1472 A. D. "Scotland received the normal church constitution, St. Andrews being raised to an archbishopric." Glasgow became a metropolitan see in 1492 A. D.[1]

Queen Margaret was the first to enter into close relations with the English church. She offered submission to Lanfranc as her spiritual father, to which he replied, "De tunc igitur sim pater tuus, et tu mea filia esto." But while her sons were ready to follow her example, they were unwilling to lose their independence thereby. Alexander I, "the Fierce," united the qualities of his father and mother. On his accession Turgot, prior of Durham and father confessor of Queen Margaret, was elected to the see of St. Andrews as one likely to carry out her plans, and was consecrated in 1109 A. D. He tried, but failed, to bend Alexander to his will, and on his death a successor was sought from Canterbury, in the hope of escaping the pretensions of York through the rivalry of the two sees.[2] Eadmer was sent, who sought, but failed, to subordinate St. Andrews to Canterbury. As Alexander would not let Turgot go to Rome, so

[1] Norman Conq., IV, pp. 349, 357, note; Makower, Const. Hist., p. 108.
[2] H. and S., Counc., II, Pt. I, pp. 155, 170. Canterbury claimed jurisdiction over Britain through the bull of Gregory I to Augustine. York claimed jurisdiction over Scotland "on account of the signature of Wilfrith at the council of Rome, and the short episcopate of Trumwin over the Scots." (Early Kings, I, p. 178.)

Eadmer should not go to Canterbury as bishop of St. Andrews. He finally resigned, but after eighteen months wished to be reinstated (1122). He wrote to Alexander:

> I entreat you not to believe that I wish to derogate in any way from the liberty or dignity of the Scottish kingdom; since if you still persist in retaining your opinion about your former demands in respect of the King of England, the Archbishop of Canterbury, and the sacerdotal Benediction (an opinion with which I would not then concur, from entertaining ideas which, I have since learnt, were erroneous), you shall find that I will no longer differ from your views, nor will I let these questions separate me from God's service, and from your love that in all things I may follow out your will.

Alexander refused to restore him, however, and appointed Robert, Prior of Scone, to the see (1123). In the diocese of Glasgow Earl David (Earl, 1107–24) appointed his tutor John as bishop. He soon fled from his unruly flock, but returned later consecrated by Paschal II. Thorstein, archbishop of York, having triumphed over Canterbury for the time, summoned John, and suspended him when he refused to acknowledge the dependence of Glasgow on York. John's appeal to Rome was not settled till 1174, when Alexander III made Glasgow "specialem filiam nostram nullo mediante."[1]

These conflicting claims gave rise to a great many complications. Political and ecclesiastical jurisdiction over certain districts often rested in different persons. These relations were constantly changing, and there was every opportunity for asserting claims, which were without foundation, to temporal as well as ecclesiastical supremacy. The chroniclers were monks, who were likely to be more familiar with ecclesiastical than with temporal jurisdiction, and to infer that the former carried the latter with it. Such changes doubtless did arise in course of time. It is necessary to remember the spirit and ultimate outcome of the entire struggle in order to keep one's bearings, and to form a correct estimate of the relations between the two kingdoms.

[1] Eadmer, Hist. Nov., Bk. 6; Early Kings, I, pp. 174, 181–2, note.

During Edgar's reign over Scotland another strand was added to the bonds that were knitting the kingdoms together. Editha, the daughter of Malcolm and Margaret, became the wife of Henry I of England. With this exception, and the defeat of an invasion on the north, the reign of Edgar was uneventful and colorless. He died in 1107 A. D., bequeathing to his brother Alexander the main part of the kingdom, but leaving Scottish Cumbria to David, who was his favorite brother. The expression in the chronicle, "Alexander his brother succeeded to the kingdom, as King Henry granted him," is a reminder of the family, rather than of the feudal, relation which existed between the two crowns, and seems to imply Alexander's desire for the moral support which his brother-in-law's confirmation would give, rather than Henry's desire to assert a feudal claim to overlordship. The risings, which Alexander had to put down with a stern hand, certainly give color to this view.[1] Florence of Worcester and Simeon of Durham both note Alexander's accession, but are absolutely silent regarding any concession of rights by Henry I, or of homage by Alexander. The later relations between Henry and the brothers of his queen clearly show that he made no effort to limit their independence, or to obtain homage except for fiefs which were granted them in England. Alexander married Sybilla, a natural daughter of King Henry, who seems, however, to have had little to commend her.[2] The chief interest of his reign lies in his contest with, and triumph over, the English church, in so far as that contest affected his rights as an independent king.[3] That he apparently accomplished little else of general interest should not be laid at his door. The kingdom had been disorganized since the death of Malcolm III. The reigns of Duncan, Donald, and Edgar had been little better than an interregnum, so far as the development of a national kingdom was concerned

Edgar,
1097–1107 A.D.

Alexander,
1107–1124 A.D.

---

[1] A.-S. Chron., Hen. Hunt., An. 1107; Early Kings, I, pp. 170 ff.; Hailes' Annals, I, p. 56.

[2] Early Kings, I, p. 183, note.   [3] See above.

The seeds planted by Alexander could not bear their fruit at once. On his death in 1124 A. D. without heirs, his brother David succeeded him, uniting again the entire kingdom under one rule.¹ David was the first to sustain the double office of Scottish king and English baron. He had visited the English court, and was thoroughly acquainted with all its ways.² While still earl, he grants a charter, interesting as the first of many documents of a similar nature, addressed "to Edward the reeve, and all his successors, and all his men of his land and soke in London and Totenham."³

David, 1114-1153 A. D.

David had married Matilda, daughter of Earl Waltheof of Northumberland and widow of Simon de St. Liz. Of the vast estates to which she was heiress Northumberland had been retained by the crown, since the forfeiture of Robert de Mowbray. Northampton had been conferred on St. Liz, as the honor of Huntingdon was on David. It would seem, from the Chronicle, that David was also earl of Northampton, but he was probably simply guardian of the younger St. Liz, who is found in possession on the death of David, in 1153.⁴ David is the brother of Matilda, queen of England, the husband of Waltheof's daughter Matilda, the uncle of Matilda, wife of Stephen of Blois, and of Matilda, daughter of Henry I, the Empress-Queen. It is not strange, therefore, to find the relations between the two kingdoms very friendly, with no mention of feudal rights on either side. The Pipe Roll of Henry I makes frequent mention of the corrody for the entertainment of the king of Scotland in coming to the king's court in England and returning from England to Scotland—in Nottingham and Derby shires, in Yorkshire, Northumberland, and Durham.⁵ To

Claims to Northumberland

and Huntingdon

---

¹ Sim. Dun., Hist. Reg., II, p. 275.   ² Celtic Scot., I, p. 454.

³ Bain, Cal. Docts., I, No. 2; W. Malms., Gest. Reg., Bk. V, § 400.

⁴ A.-S. Chron., An. 1124. On distinction between honor and earldom, *cf.* Early Kings, II, p. 411, note; also I, pp. 187-8, note.

⁵ Bain, Cal. Docts., I, Nos. 3, 4, 6, 9, 11, 14, 23, 24.

Fulco, of Hertfordshire, is pardoned ten marks of silver "for love of the K. of Scotland." The sheriffs of Cambridge, Huntingdon, Northampton, Bedford, and Lincoln (cerchetone wapentac) shires render their account "in pardon by the K.'s writ; to the K. of Scotland"—pounds or shillings. So also with the county of Rutland and the "Four Sheriffs" of London. The sheriffs of London and Middlesex render account of "the city aid;" of "the Dane-geld;" and for "a murder in the hundred and half of Edelmeton (Edmonton?);" all to the king of Scotland.[1] During a long and glorious reign, David's grace and force of character, together with his consummate tact, were no less conspicuous than his powerful connections and extensive dominions.

Henry began his efforts to secure the succession while in Normandy in 1115 A. D., by requiring of the chief men there homage and oaths of fealty to his son William. The following year he did the same in England, calling a great "Conventio optimatum et baronum totius Angliae apud Searesberiam." But the sinking of the White Ship, on her return from Normandy in 1120, frustrated all his efforts and left him without a son. He, therefore, sought to secure as his successor his daughter Matilda, whose husband, the Emperor Henry V, had just died. Such

Relations with Henry I — succession was an innovation, and David, now king of Scotland, seems to have taken an active and influential part in Henry's plans, and in forwarding the interests of his niece.[2] He was in England during the year 1126, and met in the following year with all the chief clergy and laity of England in the Christmas *gemot* at Windsor, where archbishops, bishops, abbots, earls, and thanes swore allegiance to Matilda. She then passed over to Normandy, where she was married to Geoffrey of Anjou (1127). David was the first to swear allegiance to Matilda, but it was as an English baron and not as king of Scotland.[3] Alexander had not been present at

[1] Bain, Cal. Docts., I, Nos. 15–20, 22, 25, 28.
[2] A.-S. Chron., An. 1115, 1126; Fl. Wig., Sim. Dun., Hist. Reg., An. 1116.
[3] W. Malmes., Hist. Nov., Bk. I, §§ 452, 460.

the earlier "Conventio," as would have been the case had he been the liegeman of Henry. Mr. Robertson well says: "The absence of the elder brother, who held no lands in England, from the earlier council, and the presence of the younger, who held the Honor of Huntingdon, at the later, distinctly mark that the homage must have been performed for fiefs in England. When there were no fiefs held, no homage was required."[1]

Eight years later (1133) Henry died, and Stephen, who had contended with Robert of Gloucester for precedence in swearing allegiance to Matilda, usurped the crown. At the same time David crossed the border with an army, and, seizing strongholds in Cumberland and Northumberland as far as Durham (with the exception of Bamborough), received hostages and oaths of fealty on behalf of his niece from the barons of that region. Stephen soon advanced to the north, and David fell back on Newcastle. The kings met soon after. David refused to hold anything of Stephen, in violation of his oath to Henry I, but permitted his son, Prince Henry, to do homage to Stephen at York, and to receive, in addition to the honor of Huntingdon, Doncaster and Carlisle, with all which pertained to them. The strongholds which had been taken by David[2] were given back, with the exception of Carlisle, and it was agreed, "*as some say who were present* at this convention," that if Stephen granted Northumberland to anyone, the claims of Prince Henry to it should take precedence over all others, and receive just consideration in the *curia* of the king. From this time the kings of Scotland place this claim in the foreground, as part of their settled policy. They are careful to perform homage and service in due form for their English fiefs, lest by forfeiture they should lose their right to this valuable claim. Prince Henry accompanied Stephen to the south, but the preference shown him there by the king roused the jealousy of Ranulph of Chester and others, whose rude conduct caused the indignant

and Stephen

---

[1] Early Kings, II, p. 403.

[2] A.-S. Chron., An. 1135-6; J. and R. Hex., An. 1135-6. Among the castles taken by David were Carlisle, Werk, Alnwick, Norham, and Newcastle.

David to recall his son. Nor would he allow him to return to the English court, though he was often summoned.

There are several reasons which explain David's apparent acquiescence in Stephen's usurpation. The English barons, almost without exception, failed to rally around Matilda, and David was not so unwise as to attempt to support her cause alone. Stephen's wife was also David's niece, and he might well be perplexed in trying to reconcile duty with inclination. For the difference in character between the two Matildas seems to have been wholly in favor of Stephen. Malmesbury assigns David's action to his conciliatory character, his advancing years, and a desire for ease and quiet.[1] But this is not consistent with his later conduct. It seems probable, finally, that he was not blind or deaf to self-interest, though he sets a shining and exceptional example of fidelity to his feudal oath — a fidelity which was soon to be put in strong contrast by the faithlessness of Matilda's son, Henry II, to David's grandson, Malcolm IV.

A detailed account of the northern campaigns and of the battle of the Standard, though very interesting, is not essential to the present discussion.[2] The results, however, are of great importance. As the outcome of the first movement Prince Henry does homage for Doncaster and Carlisle, and his claims to Northumberland are promised consideration. In 1137 David again entered Northumberland, while Stephen was in Normandy. At the request of Thurstin, archbishop of York, a truce was agreed to till Stephen should return to England. On his return messengers were sent from the king of Scots, demanding that Northumberland should be given to Prince Henry. This being refused, the truce was broken off, the castle of Werk was besieged, and finally forced to surrender; Northumberland was devastated and the castle of Norham taken. David then advanced into Yorkshire. The barons of this region had as yet remained neutral, waiting to see which party would be vic-

[1] Hist. Nov., Bk. I, § 462.
[2] See J. and R. Hex., Hen. Hunt., Athel. Abbot of Rievaulx; *cf.* also Early Kings, Vol. I.

torious. But now that their own safety and wealth were threatened, they took up arms. Robert de Bruce and Bernard de Balliol met David and urged him for old friendship's sake, and for the common good, to cease his warfare, offering to Prince Henry at the same time the earldom of Northumberland. But David, perhaps knowing they could not carry out their agreement, refused to yield to their entreaties, and they returned to their allies—Robert having first renounced his allegiance to David and the fief he held of him in Galloway, and Bernard the fealty he had recently sworn to him. The battle of the Standard, at North Allerton, in the North Riding of Yorkshire, soon followed. David's defeat was largely due to the unruly character of a part of his host. "The custom of 'Scottish service,' which bound every man to attend 'the hosting' across the frontier, swelled the ranks of the army with a body of men, fierce and warlike indeed, and endued with that self-willed and reckless courage which has on more than one occasion been their bane, but often indifferently armed, and as undisciplined as they were unruly."[1] His plans, which were skillfully made from his large experience in English affairs and in the methods of feudal warfare, were rendered useless by the mutinous demand of the wild men of Galloway and others, that they, though unprotected against the mail-clad Norman chivalry and the terrible English arrows, should lead the van in the charge on their hereditary foes. Their repulse and the eventual defeat of the disorganized Scottish forces followed as a matter of course.[2] David, however, soon gathered his scattered troops and again marched southward. But the advent of Alberic, the papal legate to England, offered another opportunity for mediation, in which David's niece, the wife of Stephen, joined. In the spring of 1139, at Durham, Northumberland was granted to Prince Henry in addition to his other fiefs, in the presence of the earls and barons of England, many of whom, in accordance with the treaty, did

---

[1] Early Kings, I, p. 208. By old custom every freeman must attend the hosting once a year.

[2] J. and R. Hex., An. 1137-8; Fl. Wig., II, p. 111.

homage to him for their lands, saving only their fealty to Stephen. Stephen was to retain Bamborough and Newcastle, for which an equivalent was to be given Henry in the south. The treaty, which had been made between Matilda and Prince Henry, was confirmed by Stephen at Nottingham in 1139, and their relations were now not only friendly, but intimate."[1] King

with the Empress Matilda

David, however, remained faithful to the empress-queen, and rendered her material assistance after Stephen's surrender at Lincoln and her subsequent rise to power. But her proud and harsh manner alienated her supporters, and David was forced to flee with her in the rout at Winchester, retiring once more to his own kingdom.

In 1149 a new combination was formed. The son of Matilda and Geoffrey, soon to be Henry II, came to Carlisle to

and Her Son

be knighted there by David in the presence of Prince Henry and Ranulph, earl of Chester. The dispute between the prince and Ranulph over Carlisle and Cumberland was now settled.[2] Ranulph did homage to King David and received in lieu of his claims on Carlisle the honor of Lancaster, agreeing also that his son should take a wife from the daughters of Prince Henry. Stephen, suspecting the true nature of this meeting, came to York. It had been agreed that David, Henry of Normandy, and Ranulph should meet at Lancaster, uniting their forces in an attack on Stephen. David, faithful as ever to his oath, advanced on Lancaster with the young Henry But the faithless Ranulph failed to appear, the plan came to nothing, and Henry returned to Normandy.[3] Hoveden says:

Henry, son of the Empress Matilda, now a youth of sixteen years of age, having been brought up at the court of David, king of Scots his mother's uncle, was knighted by the same King David, at the city of Carlisle, having first given his oath that if he should come to be king of England, he would restore to him Newcastle and the

---

[1] J. and R. Hexham, An. 1138-9.
[2] *Ibid*, An. 1140; Freeman, Wm. Rufus, II, p. 549.
[3] J. Hexham, Hen. Hunt., An. 1149.

whole of Northumbria, and would allow him and his heirs to hold forever in peace, without challenge of their rights, the whole of the land which lies between the rivers Tweed and Tyne.[1]

William of Newburgh says the same in substance. Both these men were English monks. As authorities they take first rank. There seems no reason, therefore, to doubt these statements. They both lived in the reign of Henry II. Hoveden was a clerk in his court, and was sent north on a mission to Galloway. They had every facility for knowing the facts, and no reason for distorting them. The silence of other English chroniclers on this point is easily explicable. Henry, therefore, acknowledged David's claims in the north of England, and solemnly promised to protect them, should he come to the throne.

David was now at the height of his power. He and his son held a kingdom more closely bound together than ever before. It extended to the Tyne and practically included Cumberland, Westmoreland, the honor of Huntingdon, Northumberland, and Doncaster. He was overlord in the honor of Lancaster. He made a grant of Furness in Westmoreland, and decided claims "in honorem de Sciptun et Crafna" far south of the Tees in York, without consulting the wish or prerogative of the English king.[2] But the death of his only son, Prince Henry, in 1152, frustrated his plans. Of an attractive face and figure, manly, forceful, and winsome in character, beloved by English as well as Scots, Henry would undoubtedly have carried on his father's work, and have maintained, if he did not increase, the relative power of the northern kingdom. The unity and prosperity of Scotland at this period, as opposed to the impoverished and desolated condition of England, make the latter not impossible. Of Henry St. Bernard said: "A brave and noble soldier, he walked like his father in the paths of justice and of truth."[3] The abbot of Rie-

David's Power. Death of His Son

---

[1] Newb. Hist. Ang., Hoveden, An. 1148-9. *Cf.* Introds. to above, statements of Hardy and Stubbs.

[2] J. of Hexham, An. 1151; Early Kings, I, p. 222.

[3] Quoted in Early Kings, I, p. 225.

vaulx, in more extravagant, but perhaps no less sincere language, exalts the merits of one who was his personal friend. David lost no time in securing the succession to Henry's sons, Malcolm and William. The former was sent through all the parts of Scotland to be acknowledged as the king's successor, while the king himself went with William to Northumberland to secure his acceptance as overlord by the English barons.[1] Meanwhile Matilda's son Henry arrived in England from Normandy, and Stephen took the opportunity afforded by the death of David's son to grant the honor of Huntingdon to the earl of Northampton, hoping thus to strengthen his own cause.[2]

David's Death, 1153 A. D. Not long after, David also died. In opposition to the sterner measures of his brother Alexander, he made conciliation the keynote of his whole policy. Under his able rule, and through his careful oversight of agriculture and of industry in general, Scotland became the "granary of England" during this troubled period. He encouraged the advent of knights and nobles of foreign birth, using them as a balance between his Gaelic and Norman followers. Mr. Freeman says of David: "He was the creator of the more recent kingdom, the strengthener of its ecclesiastical and feudal elements." And of Northumberland and Cumberland: "The grant of these earldoms to a Scottish king, or to a Scottish king's son, practically amounted to cutting them off from the kingdom of England." This strikes the keynote of the entire history. Scotland was always, at least in spirit, an aggressive, independent kingdom, pushing her borders southward into English territory, where she was not without good claims to inheritance. Had David been followed by a strong ruler, the Tyne and not the Tweed might have continued for years to mark the southern limit to the overlordship of the Scottish king.[3]

Neither Freeman nor Lingard cites authority for saying that

[1] J. of Hexham, W. Newb., An. 1152.
[2] Lytt. Hist., II, p. 243.
[3] William of Newburgh (Bk. I, Cap. XXII) says: "Aquilonalis vero regio, quae in potestatem David regis Scottorum usque ad flumen Tesiam cesserat, per ejusdem regis industriam in pace agebat." *Cf.* Early Kings, I, p. 227.

David claimed Cumberland as having anciently belonged to the heir apparent of the Scottish throne. The only claim made was for Northumberland, and this, says Mr. Robertson, "was waived at the time for the fiefs of Carlisle and Doncaster."[1] There is absolutely no mention of Cumberland, nor any allusion to any right of inheritance there. The grant of Doncaster might as justly be taken to imply an ancient right in the south of York, as the grant of Carlisle an ancient right in Cumberland. What is known as Cumberland had been ceded to Malcolm II by Edmund in 945 A. D. But it had been withdrawn on the death of Malcolm, and from 1070 to 1092 Malcolm III had held it by right of conquest. Then William Rufus invaded it and fortified Carlisle. Henry I granted this district of Carlisle, as an earldom, to Ranulph le Meschines, who gave it up in 1118 for the earldom of Chester. It then remained in the hands of the crown till granted to David. Before the death of Henry I, however, it was divided into the shires of Carlisle and Westmoreland. The modern county of Cumberland does not appear as such in the Pipe Rolls till 1177. Mr. Freeman says: "Cumbrian geography is one of the most mysterious of subjects, and it may be discreet to abstain from searching over narrowly into the exact relations between the territory which was now granted to Henry and the territory which had been in the old time granted to Malcolm." The expression "discreet" is a decided concession to the Scottish claims.[2]

[1] Freeman, Norman Conq., V, pp. 256, 260-1; Lingard, Hist. Eng., II, p. 69; Early Kings, I, p. 193, note. The whole subject is placed in a false light by Fordun's effort to put Cumberland on the same basis as Huntingdon in relation to the two crowns — an effort for which there is no historical basis.

[2] Norman Conq., V, p. 261; Wm. Rufus, II, p. 545; Early Kings, I, p. 194, note. The simple reason, says Mr. Freeman, why Cumberland and Westmoreland do not appear in the Domesday survey, is that they formed no part of England under the Conqueror. They were all border lands, and treated more as hostile territory than as integral parts of England. So much of them as did belong to the kingdom was included under Yorkshire. Even under Wm. Rufus there was no earldom of Cumberland. It was the district of Carlisle.

CHAPTER IV.

THE REIGN OF THE FIRST PLANTAGENET.

The death of Stephen left Malcolm "the Maiden," a boy of thirteen, face to face with his powerful neighbor, Henry II. Malcolm's father had without doubt possessed Northumberland, and the chronicles are quite agreed that on Malcolm's accession to the throne his brother William "the Lion" became earl of Northumberland.[1] Henry's policy was to reduce or destroy the power of the nobles, which had grown so rapidly during Stephen's reign. He was ambitious, and utterly unscrupulous, if necessary, in order to attain his ends. Forgetful of the oath he had sworn, he waited only long enough to secure himself on the throne and to bring some order out of the chaos that had reigned, before he demanded from the young Malcolm all the northern counties which his father and grandfather had held. Of the contracting parties Henry alone survived. Matthew of Westminster says that Malcolm, having invaded England in a hostile manner and rashly occupied what did not belong to him, was repelled by Henry with force, to whom the king of Scotland then surrendered Carlisle, the castle of Bamburgh, Newcastle on the river Tyne, and the whole of the county of Laudon; while Henry restored to Malcolm the earldom of Huntingdon.[2] There is no evidence of such an invasion, however. It would have been most ill-advised — for Malcolm had nothing to gain and everything to lose. That he reluctantly yielded to Henry's demand, and surrendered the counties, in the enjoyment of which the king had

Henry II, 1154-1189 A. D.
Malcolm IV, 1153-1165 A. D.

The Northern Counties

---

[1] Hoveden, An. 1153; J. of Hexham, Nic. Trivet., W. of Newb., An. 1152; Rad. Dic., An. 1173.
[2] An. 1157.

solemnly sworn to assure him, is undoubted. At the same time he advanced his claims on, and received investiture for, the honor of Huntingdon, for which he did homage.[1] The question now arises whether *Lothian* was included in his surrender. The earlier and better authorities, with one exception, are silent regarding it. Triveti includes "civitatem Carlioli, villamque Novi-castri super Tynam, castrumque Bamburgiae cum territorio adjacente," and says Henry restored to Malcolm the earldom of Huntingdon. William of Newburgh mentions only "Northumbriam, Cumbriam, Westmeriam." Hoveden says Malcolm met the English king at Chester "et homo suus devenit, eo modo quo avus suus fuerat homo veteris regis Henrici, salvis omnibus dignitatibus suis" (An. 1157).[2] Roger of Wendover, however, adds "totum comitatum Lodonensem," which Matthew of Westminster calls the county of Laudon. They are supported in this statement by Ralph of Diceto. He was born not later than 1130, probably in France, where he also studied. But much of his life was spent in England, and the amalgamating forces at work there made him an Englishman. He became high dean of St. Pauls in 1180. His work as a chronicler began late in life. "In the roll of English historians of the twelfth century no name stands higher" than his.

and Huntingdon

It was this high authority which Wendover copied in proof of the fact that Lothian was surrendered to Henry. But Diceto, it seems, was not an original authority. He drew his materials from a still earlier writer. "The obligations of our author to Robert de Monte," says Mr. Stubbs, "are unquestionable."

[1] Walt. Heming., W. Newb., An. 1156-7. Homage always *preceded* the conferring of fiefs. Where its nature or extent was in dispute, it was often tendered in general terms with a reservation by one or both of the parties — *cf.* the case of Edward III and Philip of France, as also that of Edward I and Alexander III. A similar policy was followed in the vague statement of boundaries in some of the early treaties of the United States. Napoleon once remarked of the boundaries in the Louisiana cession that if the stipulation "was not somewhat vague already, it would perhaps be politic to make it so." (Winsor, Nar. and Crit. Hist. America, VII, p. 479; Early Kings, II, p. 405 ff.; Kitchen, Hist. France, I, p. 405; II, pp. 15, 36.)

[2] Early Kings, I, p. 353, note; II, p. 407, note.

The abbey of Mont-Saint-Michel was "one of the four great centers to which pilgrims flocked from distant parts of Europe." Its abbot, Robert, died in 1186. Though a foreigner, his work is considered "essential for the due comprehension of the reign of Henry the Second." He visited England a number of times in the interests of abbey lands there. At Mont-Saint-Michel he met the leading men of the time, and acquired a wide range of information. His chronicle forms the basis for Ralph of Diceto to 1171, possibly as late as the year 1183.[1] Thus from the *scriptorium*, or writing room, of Saint-Michel came the sources of Diceto, who, in turn with Robert de Monte, supplied the materials for the *scriptorium* of St. Albans. A clue is thus afforded as to the origin of the story about the cession of Lothian — a cession of which the best authorities are ignorant, and which is incompatible with the later history. In 1153, the date of King David's death, Robert says Malcolm succeeded to the kingdom of Scotland, while his brother received "comitatum Lodonensem." The English chronicles are equally definite in saying that William was established as earl of Northumberland. Again, in 1157, Robert says Malcolm surrendered "comitatum Lodonensem" and other lands to Henry, and the best English sources are again agreed that he surrendered the three counties of Northumberland, Cumberland, and Westmoreland. Robert does not mention Northumberland. Yet it certainly was transferred at this time. It seems clear, therefore, that the "comitatum Lodonensem" in which William was established as earl by his father David, in 1153, is the same as the "comitatum Lodonensem" surrendered to Henry II four years later, and was nothing else than the county of Northumberland. The entire course of the history forbids the supposition that both Lothian and Northumberland were included, at this period, under the common name of either district alone. Diceto copied Robert de Monte as he found him.[2] In the thirteenth century these

---

[1] Robt. De Torig. and Rad. de Diceto, Introds., Howlett and Stubbs. *Cf.* Early Kings, II, p. 427, on Diceto. The passage relating to the cession of Lothian is regarded as an interpolation.

[2] The grossest errors were thus originated or perpetuated. Fl. Wig. (An. 974) says

chronicles were embodied in the work of the monks of St. Albans, who now eagerly seized on anything which placed Scotland in a dependent relation to England. "Comitatum Lodonensem" could mean nothing else to their minds than Lothian. The legendary account of its cession in 975 was embellished with the feudal details of a later age, and, linked with this fabrication recession by Malcolm IV, was handed down for Edward I to use in establishing his legal and *historical* claim to overlordship in the kingdom of Scotland![1] It is significant that no writer has yet explained, or attempted to explain, how Lothian, if it *was* given up to Henry by Malcolm IV, reappears in possession of the Scottish crown. With the growth of the Exchequer and other court records, such matters were carefully noted. Yet there is nothing to indicate that Lothian was either granted or held as a fief of the English crown. Everything points to the conclusion that it was not given up by Malcolm, and that it formed a part of the independent kingdom of Scotland.

The Pipe Rolls of Henry II first mention Malcolm IV in 1157. Lincolnshire renders account "for the corrody of the K. of Scotland, 72l. 19s. 10d." In the same shire the sheriff

---

Eadgar had a fleet of 3,600 ships, 1,200 each on the east, north, and west coasts of Britain. Matt. Paris, copying Fl. Wig., adds a fleet of 1,200 on the south, but retains the total of 3,600! On the *scriptorium* see Hardy, Cat. Brit. Hist., Vol. III, pp. x, xxxv ff.

[1] He appealed to Diceto in 1292, and valued his work so highly that he caused "the insertion on its blank pages of the official documents touching the submission of the competitors for the Scottish crown to his sovereign arbitration." (Stubbs, Introd. Rad. de Dic., II, p. lviii.) The St. Albans chroniclers brand the cession of 975 as false by the very language they employ and the usages they describe. For feudalism was not full-blown in England in the middle of the tenth century, either in its institutions or language. Yet they ascribe to the reign of Edgar the characteristic feudal features of their own times. Mr. Robertson says, "The addition of Wendover with the *mansiones*, held to the days of the second Henry, was purposely framed to correspond with the supposed cession of Lothian, which the same chronicler has added to the fiefs surrendered by Malcolm IV to the English king in 1157; a cession which has not only been overlooked by every contemporary authority, but was also totally ignored by the English kings themselves, who showed an unaccountable negligence in exercising the right, which they would unquestionably have acquired by such an act, of summoning the baronage of the Lothians to perform the military service due to their English overlord." (Rog. Wend., An. 975; Early Kings, II, p. 392.)

accounts for murders; "in the land of the K. of Scotland 2s. 4d." Yorkshire has a corrody of 123l. 0s. 9d. for sixteen days, and renders account of the Danegeld "in the land of the K. of Scotland, 17l. 8s." In Nottingham and Derby shires, "in discharge of the K.'s corrody at Pech (the Peak of Derbyshire) by Nigel de Broc, 10l. 16d. And at Nottingham and Pech, 37l. 12s. 3d. by the king's writ. And paid for wine at Pech, 72s., by the K.'s writ."[1] Perhaps it was here, in the midst of hunting and other festivities, that Henry persuaded Malcolm to yield to his demands.

This same year (1157) finds Malcolm in possession in Northamptonshire. The next year the sheriffs of Middlesex render their accounts; "to the K. of Scotland 3s. 4d.;" in Northamptonshire, "4l. 7s. 9d. on his domains;" in Rutland, 9s. 6d.[2] In Yorkshire, "William de Sumerville owes 20 marks of silver; but he remains in the land of the K. of Scotland in Lothian" (sed manet in terra regis Scotiae in Loeneis). Mr. Burton thinks this refers to Leeds in Yorkshire. The fact that Doncaster and the honor of Skipton had been controlled by King David of Scotland might give color to such a view. But the records do not at all sustain it. William owed for lands in Yorkshire. By going into Lothian he entered Scotch territory, and was no longer amenable to English jurisdiction, as he certainly would have been in Leeds and in Lothian, had Lothian been ceded with the northern counties, or been held as an English fief. This is one of the points covered by the treaty of Falaise — the mutual surrender, by either king, of fugitives from justice. The same record is repeated exactly in 1159–60. Nor is there any indication that William ever paid the 20 marks. Clearer proof could not be desired that Lothian was not at this time, as Mr. Freeman and others style it, an "English Earldom." Again, in 1163–4, accounts for Norfolk and Suffolk state that "Richard the moneyer owes 10l., but has fled to Scotland." And in 1165, in Buckingham and Bedford shires, "Thomas the moneyer owes 2 marks, but he has fled into Scot-

[1] Bain, Cal. Docts., I, Nos. 42–6.   [2] Ibid., Nos. 48–9, 52–4.

land." In 1167 "Thomas the moneyer owes 2 marks. He has fled into Scotland and is dead."[1]

In 1158, the year following the meeting at Chester, Malcolm met Henry at Carlisle, expecting to be knighted, but for some reason the ceremony was postponed. The trouble probably was over the distinction between *liege* and *simple* homage. The latter seems to have been the usual form by which the kings of the north held their English fiefs. The former was based on military service, and Henry may now have required it of Malcolm. The young king yielded, and accompanied Henry to the siege of Toulouse —a siege "which was rendered abortive through the royal scruples about attacking a town which contained the person of his own feudal superior, the King of France."[2]

The Meeting at Carlisle. Results

Returning from Toulouse, Malcolm was knighted at Tours, and went thence to his own kingdom. While he was at Perth, a riot broke out, expressive of the native Scots' disapproval of Malcolm's policy in going to Toulouse. The king broke up the siege of the conspirators and led an army into Galloway, where the disaffection was greatest. This district enjoyed a semi-independence. It was related politically to Scotland, ecclesiastically to England. It was now thoroughly subdued, and "brought into direct feudal subjection to the Scottish crown."[3]

It is about this time (1159) that the Pipe Rolls first make mention of Malcolm's brother, William the Lion. He had inherited Northumberland from his father, but it had been surrendered by Malcolm to King Henry. Now, William de Vesci renders his account for

William the Lion

---

[1] Burton, Hist. Scot., I, p. 444, note; Bain, Cal. Docts., I, Nos. 54, 66, 68, 93, 99–100, 109. *Cf.* No. 333; Madox, Hist. of Excheq., I, p. 3. "Loeneis" was 'terra regis Scotiae" — part of the "*kingdom of Scotland*," just as "terra regis Angliae" was the kingdom of England.

[2] Hoveden, An. 1158; Triveti, An. 1159; Hailes' Annals, I, p. 117, note; Early Kings, I, p. 354, note. Edward III held the duchy of Guyenne by liege service. With the Scot kings, "The obligation of service was subsequently evaded by subinfeoffing the fief, which imposed this duty on the *Vavassor*, or tenant of the Holder-in-chief."

[3] Hoveden, An. 1159–60, Introd., p. xvi; Early Kings, I, p. 357.

Northumberland, "In pardons by the K.'s writ; in Tindale, 10l., which the brother (William) of the K. of Scotland has." This was conferred on William, says Mr. Bain, "possibly as a surrogate for the surrender of his elder brother's claims; and which, as a Liberty, was held by simple homage uninterruptedly by the Scottish kings, till confiscated by Edward I on the deposition of John de Balliol; shown by its annual recurrence in the Pipe Rolls, with one exception, when it would seem to have been temporarily seized by Henry II after William the Lion's rebellion and capture."[1]

Some years later Malcolm again set out for England, but was overtaken, while *en route*, with a serious illness. After his convalescence at Doncaster, Hoveden says "pax firma facta est inter illum et regem Angliae." The St. Albans chroniclers state that he was present at Woodstock about this time to do homage to the younger Henry, as David had done to Matilda (An. 1163), but the best authorities are silent on this point. As it was simply a repetition of homage, with a reservation of fealty to the reigning king, it could have had no special significance.[2] Malcolm died in December, 1165 A. D., at the early age of twenty-four, apparently in possession of fiefs in the shires of Cambridge, Huntingdon, Northampton, Buckingham, and Bedford.[3] The appellation of "Maiden" may have arisen on account of a delicacy of constitution inherited from Queen Margaret, but he seems never to have shown aught but a brave and sturdy spirit, entirely in keeping with that of his race.

His brother William the Lion (1165–1215) at once succeeded him in the kingdom of Scotland. The next year he either accompanied or followed Henry to Normandy. No mention is made of homage, but there seems to be no doubt that William did homage for his English holdings, hoping perhaps by his promptness in service to gain some enlargement of them in the north. There is no authority for the infer-

His Accession

---

[1] Bain, Cal. Docts., I, Nos. 64, 133; Introd., p. xvii.
[2] Palgrave, Eng. Com., II, p. cccxxxv, and Early Kings, I, p. 358, note.
[3] Bain, Cal. Docts., I, Nos. 70, 71, 85, 86, 91, 93, 95.

ence of some that William must resort to the English court to do homage for the kingdom of Scotland. He had *already entered into possession* of it. But he must do homage for the English fiefs his brother Malcolm had held, before he could receive seizin of them. Moreover, Cospatric, earl of Northumberland, died at this very juncture, and it is quite in accord with William's later efforts to conclude that his attendance on Henry was, in truth, in the hopes of recovering this coveted district. It is also worth remembering, as Mr. Eyton points out, that the duchess of Bretagne was William's sister, and that her infant daughter Constance was the object of Henry's most considerate speculations. It is evident that William possessed Huntingdon and subinfeoffed it to his brother David, who is called "Hunteduniensem comitem." The castle of Huntingdon was surrendered after William's capture in 1174. But in 1185, in a council at London, Henry "reddidet Willelmo regi Scotiae comitatum de Huntedona," though many others were offering large sums for its possession. Hoveden also says that on the death of Simon, earl of Huntingdon, the king restored (reddidet) that county to William, who straightway gave (dedit) it to his brother David. "What was *given back* must have been *taken away*, and William must have been in possession of the fief before his capture."[1]

In 1167 William de Vesci renders account from Northumberland. "In lands granted to the brother[2] of the K. of Scotland, 10l. in Tindale. . . . . Kiohher, the 'man' of the K. of Scotland, owes 1 mark for failure in coming before the justices. Turchil Cadiol owes 2 marks for same plea. Adam de Nunnewic owes 40s. for same plea." Had *Lothian* been an English earldom, the sub-tenants might have been summoned before the justices and fined, as they were in Northumberland. The record

[1] Bain, Cal. Docts., I. No. 107; Itinerary of Hen. II, p. 92; Wm. Newb., Lib. II, Cap. 31, 37; Ben. Pet., Rog. Hov., An. 1166, 1184-5; Early Kings, I, p. 362; Hailes' Annals, I. p. 124, notes.

[2] This expression occurs from 1167 to 1171, when it is changed to "the king of Scotland." William probably continued to hold the fief after he became king, though the form of the account was not changed till 1171.

is repeated in 1168, and in 1169 these "men of the K. of Scotland in Tindale account for 6 marks; pardoned by the K.'s writ to the K. of Scotland himself, 6 marks, and he is quit." William also has fiefs in Buckingham and Bedford shires, in Cambridge and Huntingdon, in Northampton, Warwick, and Leicester shires. Rutland reappears in 1169. Richard de Humez renders account of "10s. 2d. for murders of Wrangedich hundred; in pardons by the K.'s writ to the K. of Scotland, 5s. 10d., and he owes 4s. 4d. He also accounts for 26s. 6d. for the amercement of the wapentake of Roteland; in pardon to the K. of Scotland 26s. 6d."[1]

But as long as the hereditary claims of his family in Northumberland were not conceded, William was dissatisfied. No open breach occurred, however, and in 1170 he and his brother David, earl of Huntingdon, were present at the coronation of the younger Henry, where they took the oath of fealty to him, saving their allegiance to his father.[2]

The struggle with the church had now reached its climax in the murder of Becket. Louis VII had also become hostile again, regarding it as an insult that his daughter Margaret, who had married the younger Henry, had not been crowned with him. The ceremony was, therefore, repeated in 1172, at Winchester. Soon after, at the instigation of Louis, Henry demanded of his father either England or Normandy as his portion. The king refused, and the son fled across the channel to his father-in-law. A deep-laid conspiracy was soon matured. Henry had alienated many. His

Opposition to Henry II

---

[1] Bain, Cal. Docts., I, Nos. 108–9, 111, 113–123, 125–128, 130. Though Lothian and Northumberland were sometimes confused by the chroniclers, a sharp distinction seems to have been made in the king's Exchequer. That Lothian was not included in Northumberland is clear from the fact that a debtor who escaped thither was beyond the jurisdiction of the English king's treasury officials and justices, while in Tynedale he was not.

[2] Fordun, Lib. VIII, Cap. 12, 13; Ben. Pet., Rog. Hov., An. 1170. Diceto says William sought from Henry "quae in provincia Northanhimbrorum avo suo regi David fuerant donata, tradita, cartis confirmata, quae etiam fuerant ab ipso tempore longo possessa"— and that this was one of the causes which led to war. Wendover copies Diceto, but characteristically omits the phrase "cartis confirmata." (An. 1173.)

barons were discontented. He had weakened their military and judicial power by withdrawing the office of sheriff from their control. He was jealous of all authority which did not emanate from himself, and delighted to bring down the haughty pride of his nobles. Bountiful to favorites, he was unceasingly vindictive toward all who opposed his will. He was a strange combination of genius and affability, of passion and base duplicity. He reaped from his sons the harvest of which he had himself sown the seed. The love of his wife, Eleanor of Poitou, had turned to bitter hatred, and she now urged on her son, the young Henry, in his course of rebellion. Richard and Geoffrey in Aquitaine were among the disaffected. The promise of Northumberland to William the Lion made him a ready partisan in the conspiracy, while his brother David was to be confirmed in the honor of Huntingdon and to receive "in augmentum . . . . totam Cantebrigesiriam."[1] Henry sought reconciliation with Eleanor and his sons through the mediation of Louis VII and the bishops of Normandy. The prelates replied in Louis' behalf,

> He said that he had already been too often the dupe of your artifice and hypocrisy; that you had repeatedly and on the slightest pretenses, violated your most sacred engagements; and that after the experience which he had had of your duplicity, he had determined never more to put faith in your promises.

By Easter, 1173, a plot which included the kings of Scotland and France, the counts of Flanders and Boulogne, Richard, Geoffrey, and the young King Henry, besides the earl of Leicester and many of the barons in north, east, and middle England, was well under way.[2]

The king of Scotland was first in the field, crossing the border in the late summer. Depredations had apparently been begun some time earlier, judging from the story of the Pipe Rolls. In Northumberland there is account of £20 "to retain knights in the castle of Carlisle," for the damage caused by the

[1] Hoveden, Ben. Pet., An. 1172-3. "Concessit enim Willelmo regi Scotiae pro homagio et servitio suo, totam Northumberlandam usque ad Tinam."
[2] Lingard, Hist. Eng., II, p. 196; Ben. Pet., An. 1173.

Scots; also £20 each for the castle of Prudho and for Newcastle-on-Tyne; all by the writs of Richard de Luci. The abbey of Hyde in Hampshire reports "15l. of knights' scutage for the army of Scotland." From Carlisle Robert Traite " owes [is unable to pay] 27l. 6s. 6d. through the waste of the county from the war."[1] The apparent sympathy of the bishop of Durham with the rebels gave William a free passage through his territory. But on the approach of a force from the south under the king's justiciar and constable, he retired into Lothian, whither he was followed by the English forces. Diceto says a truce was asked for by William, but Hoveden and Newburgh state that it was sought by the English that they might return southward to oppose the landing of the earl of Leicester. William, apparently ignorant of the straits in which his foes were placed, granted a truce till the feast of St. Hilary. It was then renewed by him till Easter, 1174, in consideration of 300 marks which he received through the bishop of Durham — a proceeding which shows on which side the desire for a truce lay. As soon as Easter was past Earl David hastened south to command the forces of the earl of Leicester, who had been taken prisoner. King William also took the field again. He initiated a blockade of Carlisle, and, withdrawing part of his army, successfully invaded Northumberland, taking a number of castles. Returning to Carlisle he received a promise of surrender if relief did not come by Michaelmas. He then began the siege of Prudhoe castle on the Tyne, but, hearing of the approach of the Yorkshire barons, he raised the siege and began to withdraw to the north. Reaching Alnwick he invested it, but sent away to ravage the country the earls Duncan and Angus, and Richard de Moreville, " fere cum toto exercitu suo." He himself remained " cum privata familia sua." The Yorkshire barons reached Newcastle on the night of July 12, about four hundred in number. They questioned whether to proceed. But news of William's situation having reached them, they hastened on early the next

[1] Bain, Cal. Docts., Nos. 129-31.

morning. A dense fog concealed them from their enemies, who were ravaging the neighboring country, but they were in constant danger, and the more faint-hearted urged an immediate return. Bernard de Balliol, however, swore that he would not retreat, and the advance continued. The lifting fog disclosed Alnwick castle, with William and sixty of his knights tilting in a neighboring meadow. At first he took the barons for his own men, but, learning his mistake, he rode at them alone, in the most rash and foolhardy way, apparently challenging them to knightly combat. But the barons were seeking more important prizes than those of the tourney; the king's horse was slain, and he himself taken prisoner. His followers did not attempt flight, preferring a voluntary surrender to the imputation of having deserted their culpable lord and king, Wendover adds that the Scots who were slain were said to be without numbering!¹

He is Captured

Henry, meanwhile, had learned of the plan for a naval attack on England by his son and Philip, count of Flanders, and was crossing the channel from Barfleur in a storm which kept the hostile fleet at anchor in the harbor of Gravelines. On landing, he journeyed swiftly to the shrine of the martyr Becket, doing abject penance there for his sins. Passing on to London he was detained there some days by a fever, brought on by exposure and fatigue, but dispelled by the good news that William had fallen into his hands. This event dissipated the forces of the rebellion. David at once returned to Scotland, and within three weeks England was quiet. The records of the time all breathe the spirit of war. Northumberland renders account " in lands granted in Tindale which the K. of Scotland had (habuit), 10 l." The sheriff accounts for 46s. 8d. "of the issue of Aedgar Unnidering, who has gone into Scotland to the K.'s enemies." " Robert de Stuteville [Yorkshire] renders no account this year

¹ Diceto, Hoveden, Ben. Pet., An. 1173-4; Wm. Newb., Lib. II, Cap. 33. It is noticeable that Hoveden speaks of Lothian as "terram regis Scotiae," while Newburgh says of the Tweed, "quae *regnum* Anglicum Scotticumque disterminat "— statements which hardly agree with the theory that Malcolm IV ceded Lothian to Henry II with the northern counties, and that it was an English earldom.

of the farms of the county, nor of the K.'s dues therein, as he has not yet had the K.'s warrant for his expenses laid out during the war, in the K.'s service." Adam, son of Robert Truite [Carlisle], also renders no account, "as he has received nothing this year by reason of the war, as he says." Southampton again appears as fitting out the Esnecce "when she crossed the sea with the Earl of Leicester and other prisoners." Henry crossed over to Barfleur and bestowed his prisoners at Caen, August 8. A day or two later they were taken to Falaise. Peace soon followed with the king's sons and with France. At Louis' intercession most of the prisoners were released, but toward the king of Scotland Henry was inexorable. A surrender of the independence of his kingdom was the price at which William bought his freedom.[1]

[1] Ben. Pet., Hoveden, Diceto, An. 1174; Bain, Cal. Docts., I, Nos. 132–5, 137–8.

CHAPTER V.

INDEPENDENCE LOST AND REGAINED: OR, THE TREATY OF FALAISE AND THE CHARTER OF RELEASE.

On September 30, 1174, an agreement was reached between Henry, his sons, and Louis VII. This was embodied in a written manifesto, on October 30, at Falaise, where the royal family seems to have assembled, and where the state prisoners were. About the first of December William came to terms with Henry. The instrument was dated at Falaise, but the agreement was embodied in another charter, with additional witnesses, at Valognes, December 8. On the 11th the king of Scotland obtained release, and set sail for England.[1] This seems to be the true explanation of the divergence in the various authorities regarding this treaty. Hoveden and Benedict, of Peterborough, both give it.

Treaty of Falaise

Diceto has an abridged statement of it, which Mr. Robertson conclusively shows to be by a later hand than his. It mentions only two castles (Roxburgh and Berwick) to be surrendered by William, the writer being apparently ignorant "not only that Stirling, Jedburgh, and Edinburgh were also among the fortresses stipulated to be made over by the Scots, but that the latter was actually given up." The document is given in its fullest form in the Foedera, which agrees in general with the Liber Niger, except as to the number of witnesses. The Red Book of the Exchequer differs radically from the above, both in substance and in the names of witnesses. But in essentials they all agree in the following provisions:[2]

---

[1] Foedera, I, p. 37; Itinerary Hen. II, pp. 184 ff.

[2] Bain, Cal. Docts., I, No. 139; Hearne, Liber Niger, p. 36; Early Kings, I, p. 374, note; Norgate, Ang. Kings, II, p. 166, note; also Hoveden, Benedictus, and Diceto, Ad. an., I, p. 39.

The King

William was to become the liegeman of Henry for Scotland and for all his other lands.¹ He was to do fealty to to him as his liege lord, and to his son Henry, "salva fide Domini Regis patris sui," as his other "men" were wont to do.

The Church

All the bishops, abbots, and clergy of the land of the king of Scots, and of his successors, were to do fealty to the king as their liege lord at his pleasure, as his other bishops are wont to do, and to Henry, his son, and to their heirs.

William and David, his brother, with the barons and other men of the king, also conceded to Henry that the Church of Scotland should make such subjection to the Church of England as it ought, and was wont, to make in the times of the kings of England, his predecessors.

The bishops of St. Andrews and Dunkeld, with the abbot of Dunfermline and the prior of Coldingham, specially agreed that the Church of England should have that authority over the Scottish church *which by right it ought to have*, and that they would not go contrary to the right of the Church of England, and in security thereof rendered liege fealty to King Henry and his son.²

The Nobility

The earls, barons, and other men of the land of the king of Scots, at the pleasure of King Henry, were to do homage and fidelity to him as their liege lord against all men, as his other "men" were wont to do, and to his son and his heirs, *salva fide*, etc. Likewise the heirs of the king of Scots and of his barons and men were to do homage and fealty to the heirs of their lord the king, against all men.

Absentees

William and his barons pledged their faith to compel those of the barons and clergy who were absent when the treaty was made to yield allegiance and fealty to Henry, and to give such hostages as he should desire.

---

¹ Tindale seems to have been temporarily forfeited. It reappears in 1175. Some time between 1165 and 1182 William grants a charter in favor of the church of St. Mary in Furneis, Westmoreland. (Bain, Cal: Docts., I, Nos. 143, 158, 165).

² Hailes' Annals, I, pp. 130-1.

The king of Scots and his men agreed that they would receive no fugitive by reason of felony from the land of their lord the king, either in Scotland or in their other lands, unless he should be willing to come to trial in the court of his lord the king, and to abide by the judgment of the court. They were to take all such as speedily as possible, and restore them to the king or his justiciars or bailiffs in England. Similar provisions were to be enforced against fugitives from Scotland, but they might, if they chose, stand trial in the English *curia*. (This clearly marks the dependent position of Scotland at this period, and the absence of this phenomenon at all other times till Edward I as clearly marks the fact of an independent kingdom.)

Surrender of Fugitives

The new relations between the kings were not to affect the holders of fiefs under either. They were to continue to hold as they had held, and ought to hold.

Confirmation of Holdings

As a guarantee for the faithful observance and execution of this convention and fine, William was to deliver over to Henry the castles of Roxburgh, Berwick, Jedburgh, Edinburgh, and Stirling, in which English garrisons were to be maintained at the expense of the Scottish king.

Securities

He was also to deliver up as hostages his brother David, four earls, Richard de Moreville, the constable, besides barons and knights. The king and his brother were to be released as soon as the castles had been handed over, and the earls and barons as soon thereafter as they furnished lawful sons, or their nearest heirs, as hostages in their stead.

The bishops, earls, and barons also agreed that if William should seek to withdraw the allegiance he had sworn to Henry and his son, they would hold to the English king as their liege lord, against the king of the Scots and all enemies of their lord the king, the bishops promising to lay the kingdom under an interdict till William should return to his allegiance.

Thus was the subjection of the kingdom of Scotland completed. The "peace and final concord" to which William had agreed as a prisoner in chains at Falaise, in the presence of the English kings and their clergy and nobles, was now ratified in the church of St. Peter, at York, by the bishops, earls, barons, and knights of Scotland, who swore fidelity to Henry, his son, and their heirs, against all men, as their liege lords.[1] Henry availed himself of his opportunity to the utmost. Nor did he fail to exact rigorously the conditions imposed, unless for his own reasons it pleased him to remit them. To have taken the life of his captive would have been abhorrent to the moral sense of the times. Confinement would only have raised up some other Scottish leader. He acted only as William and the younger Henry would have acted, had their conspiracy been successful. He gained a forced, but distinct acknowledgment of his supremacy as over lord in the kingdom of Scotland—an overlordship of which the Chronicles give striking evidence. But, had the English kings possessed such rights of supremacy previous to this time, Henry would have gained nothing new from his captive, and the treaty of Falaise would have been a farce. If, on the other hand, the theory and claim of English overlordship be admitted, the necessity of this document shows conclusively the hitherto successful denial of and resistance to every such theory and claim by the Scots.

Scotland a dependent Kingdom

The treaty remained in force for fifteen years, during which William and his barons were often summoned by their feudal superior. Scottish kings were not strangers at the court of the kingdom in which they held fiefs. But the presence of the barons and clergy was new, and shows the changed condition of the northern kingdom.

The clergy were the first to experience the effects of the new order. The Assizes of Clarendon were re-enacted at the Council of Northampton, early in 1176. At the command of Henry, the Scottish bishops, abbots, and priors came to make their promised subjection to the English church. When it was demanded of them by the king, they replied that their predeces-

[1] Hoveden, Aug. 10, 1175.

sors had never owed any such subjection, neither ought they to render it. Roger of York insisted on his claims, specially over the bishops of Glasgow and Candida Casa, adducing as proofs the papal bulls he held in his hand. Contention over the disputed jurisdiction of Canterbury and York at once grew hot. Jocelyn, bishop of Glasgow, declared his see was "the special daughter of the Roman church,"[1] and was now exempt from all subjection by archbishops or bishops, whatever its previous relation to York. Either at the instigation of the archbishop of Canterbury, who hoped thus to gain the submission of the Scottish clergy to his see, or because the king dreaded to arbitrate in a very complicated dispute, Henry dismissed the clergy of the north, "nulla subjectione facta Anglicanae ecclesia."[2]

The Church Escapes Subjection

In 1180 a new dispute arose, in which William took a leading part. The bishop of St. Andrews died, and the canons of the church elected John Scot as his successor. But William had elected his chaplain, Hugh, to the position and ordered him to be consecrated by the bishops of the kingdom. John appealed to Rome, and Alexander III sent his subdeacon, Alexius, to learn the merits of the case. He at length deposed Hugh and caused John to be confirmed and consecrated. William apparently acquiesced in this decision, but immediately after the consecration he banished John from the kingdom. During the struggle Roger, archbishop of York, was appointed papal legate, with power to lay the kingdom of Scotland under an interdict if William remained obdurate. The king would not yield. The sentence of banishment was renewed against John and his uncle, bishop of Aberdeen, who fled to Henry in Normandy. William was excommunicated and his kingdom laid under an interdict. Pressure was also brought to bear on Henry, who summoned William to Normandy to answer the complaints of the bishops

---

[1] By bull of Alex. III, 1175; repeated by Lucius, 1182. (H. and S., Counc., II, Pt. I, pp. 40, 47.)

[2] Hoveden, Ben. Pet., An. 1176. See Bain, I, No. 147, for the forged letter of William to Alex. III, urging the claims of York.

(1181). It was then agreed that Matthew should be restored to his see. John was to give up St. Andrews, but was to have any other bishopric he chose, with the chancellorship, and forty marks annually from St. Andrews, in addition to his other revenues. The pope would not agree to this, and ordered the underclergy of St. Andrews to make submission to John as their superior, on pain of suspension. William at once expelled all who obeyed, and interdict and excommunication were renewed. The death of Alexander and Roger, a little later, opened the way to more pleasant relations with the new vicar of St. Peter, Lucius III.[1]

Henry jealously guarded against any papal interference in Scotland, looking toward a re-establishment of the kingdom on an independent basis. Nor would he permit Vivian, the legate for Scotland, to go there till he gave oath that he would do nothing against the wishes of the king. Vivian had been sent for secretly by William and his barons to settle the question of the dependence of the Scottish church on the English church. It was not till 1188, just before Henry's death, that the bull of Clement III set the matter at rest.[2]

William's capture in 1174 was no sooner assured than the unruly factions in his kingdom broke into open revolt. The chief disturbance was in Galloway. This province, since about 1100, had been ruled by Fergus, a semi-independent prince. He was conquered by Malcolm IV in 1160, and soon after retired to Holyrood Abbey, leaving his title and lands to his sons Gilbert and Uchtred, who were waiting for an opportunity to regain their former independent position. They now returned with the Scottish army from the invasion of England to their own land, destroyed the strong-

Disturbances in Scotland

---

[1] Hoveden, Ben. Pet., An. 1180-2.

[2] Hoveden, Ben. Pet.; H. and S., Counc., II, Pt. I, pp. 10, 273. Roger of York was legate for England till November, 1181. The bishop of Candida Casa, a see not among those revived by David, but apparently established by Fergus of Galloway, refused the summons of Vivian, and when excommunicated for not attending a council of Scottish bishops received shelter from his metropolitan, Roger of York. The question of disputed jurisdiction was not settled till the fourteenth century.

holds by which their subjection had been secured, drove out the men of the king of Scots, and killed the English and French there. At the same time they sent envoys to Henry with offers of their fealty. Gilbert then treacherously attacked his brother, depriving him of lands and even of life, as a result of the cruel blinding and mutilation which he inflicted. Thus, when Henry sent his chaplain, Roger of Hoveden, from Normandy to Carlisle, to negotiate with the princes of Galloway, Gilbert was sole ruler, eager to escape from William's overlordship and the almost certain punishment for his crime. As an inducement for Henry to receive him "in manu sua" he offered an annual tribute of two thousand marks of silver, and of cattle and hogs five hundred each. The envoys, however, having heard of Gilbert's cruelty, decided to refer the matter to the king, and he, either for this cause, or more probably because William had become his vassal for Galloway, refused to change Gilbert's relations with the king of Scotland.[1] As soon as the ratification of the treaty was completed at York, Henry gave William permission to retire to Scotland and to prepare an expedition against Gilbert, because of the withdrawal of his fealty and the murder of his brother. The following autumn William met Henry at Feckenham, bringing Gilbert in his train, who swore fealty, as the other Scottish barons had done, and promised him, out of the love he had for him, a thousand marks of silver. On returning to Galloway he declared the death penalty against any who should acknowledge he held his lands of the king of Scots, and kept up an intermittent ravaging of his lands. He rightly judged that Henry would not object to this thorn in the side of his chief vassal.[2]

In 1181, while William was in attendance on Henry in Nor-

[1] "Rex Scotiae et David frater ejus devenerunt ibidem homines praedicti regis de omnibus tenementis suis: et nominatim de Scotia et Galveia." (Ben. Pet., I, p. 95.) The language of the treaty is "de Scotia et de omnibus aliis terris suis." Galloway is not mentioned; nor does Lothian appear. Fergus had married an illegitimate daughter of Henry I. Hence Henry II spoke of Uchtred as "consanguineus suus."

[2] Hoveden, Pref., I, p. xvi, An. 1174-6; Also Ben. Pet., *ibid.*; Bain., Cal. Docts., I, Nos. 154, 192. Gilbert's first payment was in 1179, "8ol. 11s. by the hands of

mandy for the settlement of the quarrel about John Scot, a fresh revolt broke out in Scotland, under the lead of Donald Mac-William, a pretender to the throne. Both kings returned to England in August. But it was not till September, after the council at Nottingham, that William and his barons received permission to return to Scotland and put down the disturbance there. Three years later he was preparing an expedition against Gilbert and others who had wasted his lands, killed his men, "nec tamen cum eo pacem facere volebant."[1] But hearing of Henry's return from Normandy, he disbanded his forces and came as quickly as possible to him, with representatives of the Scottish clergy and laity. For with Henry came Matilda, daughter of Henry, duke of Saxony, whom William sought in marriage. Since the forfeiture and exile of her father, she had been with King Henry in England and Normandy. The king made no objection to the union, but the refusal of the pope to sanction the marriage, on the ground of consanguinity, is one of several indications that Henry was really unwilling to strengthen his vassal by such an alliance.[2]

The Christmas feast of 1194 witnessed the presence of William, his earls and barons, at the English court. Again, in Lent, they were summoned, with the bishops and abbots, to consider in council a papal letter regarding the relief of Jerusalem. Here, though many others offered large sums for it, Henry restored the fief of Huntingdon to William (Earl Simon having recently died), perhaps as an offset to his disappointment in not winning Matilda. William at once subinfeoffed it to his brother David.[3]

On the death of Gilbert of Galloway late in 1185, Roland,

Robert de Vallibus," of Cumberland, "and he owes 920l. 9s. . . . for having the king's benevolence." Ten years later, at Henry's death, he still owes 838l. 12s. 8d., and this sum was never paid. Robertson thinks there is some unexplained reason for Hoveden's reserve about Galloway. (Early Kings, I, p. 381, note.)

[1] Hoveden, Ben. Pet., An. 1181, 1184.

[2] Ben. Pet., An. 1184; Itinerary Hen. II, p. 62.

[3] Ben. Pet., An. 1185. Hoveden places this council in 1185, but the transfer of Huntingdon in 1184.

son of the murdered Uchtred, at once seized the territory and thoroughly subdued it. Gilbert's son Duncan was still a hostage at the English court. Henry seems at first to have passed over Roland's independent assertion of his rights, being occupied with a new marriage scheme for William the Lion.

Marriage of William the Lion The king and David, with their chief men, were summoned to the English court early in 1186. Henry received them with great courtesy and affability in order to secure their goodwill and further his plans. After some days of pleasant entertainment he proposed that William should marry Ermengarde, daughter of Richard, viscount of Beaumont.[1] After consulting his barons, William at length accepted the offer. Henry, first taking an oath from the Scottish barons that they would serve him faithfully, then sent them home again to prepare an expedition against Roland, and to bring him to the English court. Roland refused to come, and Henry, therefore, concentrated his forces on Carlisle, sending William and David to bring in the refractory usurper. But he still refused to come till hostages were given and a safe conduct granted. He then went with them and did homage to Henry for his lands, as the other Scottish barons had done, agreeing to submit the conflicting claims of Duncan to the decision of the *Curia Regis*. He also gave hostages, and William and his barons swore they would adhere to the English king if Roland proved disloyal, while the bishop of Glasgow solemnly promised on the sacred relics that he would excommunicate him if unfaithful. Roland seems to have found a refuge at the Scottish court, after the murder of his father, where he married one of William's daughters. Duncan's claims were apparently never pressed, and after the death of Henry they were given up in exchange for the earldom of Carrick. Early in September (1186) William's marriage was celebrated at Woodstock, the king giving up his palace to the royal pair. The castle of the Maidens (Edinburgh) was restored to William as a part of Ermengarde's marriage dower. After four days the bride was accompanied to

[1] Richard's father married Constance, a daughter of Henry I.

Scotland by Bishop Jocelyn and the earls and barons, William going with Henry to Marlborough.[1]

Outwardly, William seems now to have almost regained the position he occupied before his capture and the treaty of Falaise.

His Position at Henry's Death   He has fiefs certainly in Northumberland and Huntingdon. The castle of Edinburgh is again garrisoned by Scots. Jedburgh and Stirling apparently were never demanded by Henry. Only Roxburgh and Berwick remain beyond his reach, and to these he turns with longing eyes. There is no essential conflict between the narratives of Hoveden and Benedict of his efforts to regain them. According to the account of the former, Henry sent the bishop of Durham and others to collect the Saladin tithe from the kingdom of Scotland. William met them on the border and refused them entrance on such a mission, but offered to give instead to his liege lord 5,000 marks of silver, on condition that the remaining castles should be restored to him. The bishop was not empowered to complete such a transaction, and returned empty-handed to the king, who refused to accept the offer.

Benedict says that William had previously offered 4,000 marks for the castles, and that Henry had agreed to the exchange, on condition that he should receive a tenth from William's dominions. The latter "desiring to satisfy the king's petitions," conceded the tenth which he sought, *if he could persuade his men to agree to it.* But when the messengers came to collect it, they were met by the nobles and clergy and a large body of men, who swore they would never pay the tithe, even though both kings demanded it. Nor was it paid. It was the last time that Henry II would attempt to interfere in the kingdom of Scotland, for he was now fighting for his own life and dominions. On the 4th of July, 1189, he was compelled to yield. He placed himself wholly under the control and at the will of Philip, king of France, renewed his homage to him as overlord, and promised the payment of 20,000 marks. He also delivered up certain castles as security, and his barons swore

[1] Early Kings, I, pp. 387, 390, note; Ben. Pet., Hoveden, An. 1186.

that if he proved faithless, they would hold with Philip and Earl Richard against him. Humiliated, and broken-hearted over the treachery of his son, John, he died at Chinon, after an eventful reign of more than thirty-four years.[1]

Though the northern kingdom seemed to have almost recovered from the disaster of 1174, that event had really brought great changes. The king might recover the fiefs he had lost, but he could not win back the independence of the kingdom, with which his freedom had been so dearly bought. For fifteen years king, clergy, and nobles had been subject to the summons of the king of England. Their attendance at the court of Henry became a common occurrence. William's vassals were the vassals of his English overlord. Nor could he wage war against them without the consent of that overlord. These are new phenomena, which do not reappear till Edward I again assumes the overlordship of Scotland. As they mark the dependent kingdom, their absence indicates that the homage of Scottish kings was for their English fiefs, and not for the kingdom at large.

The accession of Henry's second son, Richard, brought a welcome change to Scotland. David, earl of Huntingdon, who had already been his devoted supporter, participated in the splendid coronation ceremonies, by carrying one of the three golden swords kept in the king's treasury. The absence of the king of Scotland with his barons and clergy was prophetic of the restoration of the ancient liberties of the northern kingdom. Richard was no sooner crowned than he received homage and fealty from his barons, and proceeded to put up for sale "everything he had, castles, towns and estates." Sending "mandatis urgentibus" for William, who was "invetera laborantem tristitia pro castellis," he ordered Geoffrey, archbishop-elect of York, and the barons and sheriff of Yorkshire to meet William at the Tweed,[2] and

Scotland Independent again

[1] Ben. Pet., Hoveden, An. 1188-9.
[2] W. Newburgh, An. 1189; Ben. Pet., II p. 97.
  This, again, indicates the boundary line between the two *kingdoms*. Sir Francis Palgrave says the king of Scots "held Tyndale as a regality, using therein all the

to conduct him with due honor to Canterbury. There the king of Scots did homage to Richard " pro dignitatibus suis habendis in Anglia, sicut Malcolmus frater ejus habuit." Richard then restored to William the castles of Roxburgh and Berwick, and released him and his heirs " ab ipso et regibus Angliae in perpetuum de *omnia ligantia et subjectione de regno Scotiae*." And for this "quieta clamantia fidelitatis et ligantiae de regno Scotiae," confirmed by a charter and the restoration of his castles, William gave 10,000 marks sterling.[1] Benedict of

rights of a sovereign — rights which without doubt he had equally exercised when the three lands of Cumbria, Northumbria and Westmere were placed beneath his authority. This fact is evidenced by the highly curious roll of his justices itinerant." (*Cf.* Bain, Cal. Docts., II, No. 168.) "It will appear from this roll that the king of Scots [Alexander III] exercised the powers of jurisdiction within this district exactly in the same manner as he did in Lothian, equally a portion of the Northumbrian kingdom, and held under the same allegiance. And had the northern counties continued in the possession of the Scottish crown, they would, like the lands beyond the Tweed, have had the good or ill fortune of being considered as integral portions of the Scottish kingdom." (Docts. Scot., I, p. vii.) But this roll does not mention Lothian. It applies only to Tynedale, and hence affords no evidence that Lothian was "equally a portion of the Northumbrian kingdom, and held under the same allegiance." Tynedale was held on the most generous and easy terms known to the feudal system. Yet it regularly appears in the records of the English Exchequer as a fief held by the Scottish crown. Had Lothian been held "under the same allegiance," or been aught but an "integral portion of the Scottish kingdom," as it was "*considered*" to be, it must inevitably have appeared also. When Henry III ordained "the sheriff of Northumberland . . . . and the knights of the shire . . . . to proceed to the marches between England and Scotland" to settle a dispute about them, he certainly did not consider Lothian a part of Northumberland. Nor did Hugh de Bolebec, who informed the king later that "he, with the knights of Northumberland, met in person at 'Revedeneburne' [on the Tweed] David de Lindesay, Justiciar of Lothian (Laoudie), Patric, Earl of Dunbar, and many other knights sent by the K. of Scotland." The two regions and their representatives are distinctly opposed.

[1] Mr. Bain, following Ridpath (Border Hist., p. 105, note), doubts this payment. But the evidence seems clear. In 1193-4 there is account from Westmoreland "for the carriage of the monies which were sent by the K. of Scotland, 100s." In 1199, from Yorkshire, "for the cost of carrying the treasure to London, which the K. of Scotland gave (dedit) to K. Richard, 30s." That these payments were not part of the aid contributed to Richard's ransom is evident from the next entry, under Northumberland, same year, "For 2000 marks carried from Ravendene to York, which the K. of Scotland sent to Richard, 40s." (Bain I, Nos. 221, 283-4.) Fordun (Bk. VIII) says: "Hoc anno rex magnum tenuit consilium, ubi petito ab optimatibus auxilio, promiserunt se daturos 10,000 marcas; praeter burgenses regni qui 6000 marcarum promiserunt." (*Cf.* Annals, § XXI.)

Peterborough says, "homagium pro dignitatibus suis habendis in Anglia, sicut reges Scottorum praedecessores sui habere solebant temporibus regum Angliae." The release was "*de omni ligantia et subjectione de regno Scotiae.*" Even the St. Albans chroniclers at last fall into line, and state that the homage was "de jure suo in Anglia," with release from fealty "de regno Scotiae." It seems impossible to honestly maintain that the king of Scots was not released from all homage and allegiance for his kingdom, or that he did homage to Richard for anything beyond his fiefs in England. The charter itself is as follows:

Richard by the grace of God King of England, etc. Know that we have restored to our dearest cousin William, by the same grace King of Scotland, his castles of Rokeborc and Beraich, as his own by hereditary right, to be by him and his heirs possessed forever. Moreover, we have quitted (*quietavimus*) to him all the pactions which our good father Henry King of England by new charters and by his capture extorted. On such condition, that is to say, that he do to us wholly and fully whatsoever Malcolm King of Scotland, his brother, did of right to our ancestors and of right ought to do. And we do to him whatever our ancestors of right did to the said Malcom and ought to do, to-wit, in safe conduct in coming to the court and in staying in the court and in returning from the court, and in procurations and in all liberties and dignities and honors due to him of right, according as it shall be found by four of our nobles chosen by King William himself, and by four of his nobles chosen by us. But if any one of our men shall have unjustly encroached on the marches of the kingdom of Scotland, after the said King William was taken prisoner by our father, we will that they be fully restored and brought back to the same state in which they were before his capture. Moreover, concerning his lands which he may have (*haberet*) in England, whether in demesne or in fee (*dominicis seu feodis*), to-wit, in the county of Huntedun and in all others, let him and his heirs possess them forever in the same freedom and with such custom as the aforesaid King Malcolm possessed or ought to have possessed them; unless the aforesaid King Malcolm or his heirs shall afterwards have enfeoffed any portion thereof. Provided that if any lands shall have been so enfeoffed afterwards, the services of those fiefs belong to him and his heirs. And the land which our father gave to the aforesaid King William, we will that he and his heirs perpetually possess in the same freedom in which he gave it to him. Also we have restored to him the fealties of his vassals which our father had received, and all the charters which our father had from him by means of his capture. And if perchance any shall have been retained through forgetfulness, or shall be found, we command that these be utterly without force. But the oftmentioned William has become our liege man for all the lands for which his ancestors were the liege men of our ancestors, and has sworn fealty to us and our heirs. And that this may be settled and fixed forever, we have confirmed it by this present charter and our seal.[1] (Dec. 5 1189.)

Wisdom of Richard's Policy A question may be raised as to the wisdom of Richard's policy. But if his position be considered, his action seems justified. His heart was wrapped up in the crusade. He must have money. Moreover, it would have been poor policy to leave a hostile vassal on his northern borders during his absence — a vassal irritated by the fate which had robbed his kingdom of its independence, and only waiting for an opportunity to regain it. Nor was it in accord with the policy of the Conqueror and other English kings, who preferred rather to protect their northern borders by friendly alliances than to extend their territory and jurisdiction beyond the Tweed.

The peace which continued between the two kingdoms during Richard's reign is the best justification of his policy.

The Treaty of Falaise and the Charter of Richard Compared A comparison of the treaties made by Henry and Richard with William the Lion shows that Henry extorted some service or right from William that Malcolm IV had not yielded, and that Richard restored the king of Scots to the footing he occupied before his capture at Alnwick. What Henry gained by the treaty of Falaise was a distinct acknowledgment of his overlordship in the kingdom of Scotland, with the consequent homage and service not only of the king, who was also a landholder in England, but of all his barons and clergy. This is

---

[1] Foedera, I, p. 64; Hoveden, Ben. Pet., An. 1189; Nat. MSS. Scot., I, No. XLVI.

the important feature in this treaty — the *new* right which the king of England acquired. If this be denied on the ground that Henry possessed this right previously, the treaty of Falaise is without significance. If it be affirmed that it simply restates and makes provision for the enforcement of an old right, the argument only proves that the Scottish kings had hitherto not yielded to the English claims and had maintained the independence of their kingdom. But however widely feudal *claims* and just feudal *rights* often differed, there is no evidence that Henry made any such claims, or regarded William as a rebellious vassal, except in relation to his English fiefs — of which he was temporarily deprived. He had joined as a chief conspirator in a league against the lord of those fiefs, and in doing homage for his kingdom he suffered the severest penalty which Henry could inflict. From this position of irritating and hitherto unknown dependence Richard fully released his cousin, who became his liege man for his lands in England, just as Malcolm had been the man of Richard's father — "eo modo quo avus suus [David] fuerat homo veteris regis Henrici."[1] As the dependent kingdom was clearly marked by the creation of a vassal relation between the Scottish nobles and the English king, so a renewal of independence was marked by restoration of the allegiance of William's vassals to himself. Henry had nothing to gain but homage and service for the kingdom of Scotland, and his son could give nothing else back. Any other concession would have had but a paltry value in William's eyes. Even his claims to the northern counties are allowed to drop out of sight in the presence of this greater desire. These events, therefore, indicate that the true kingdom of the Scots maintained its independence till the treaty of Falaise — an independence which was restored by the charter of Richard.

In 1190 William's brother David married Matilda, a sister of Ranulph, earl of Chester, and Richard confirmed to him the liberties of the honor of Huntingdon as his grandfather David had enjoyed them. There is some evidence that soon after

[1] Hoveden, An. 1157.

David went to the Holy Land under the banners of Richard. He, or his brother the king, held lands also in Northumberland, Warwick, Leicester, and Cambridge. But William, having regained the independence of his kingdom, was now eagerly urging his claims in the north of England. He had remained loyal to the king in his absence and captivity. He had contributed 2000 marks toward his ransom.[1] Earl David had participated in the siege of Nottingham — which John's partisans refused to give up — and also in the council which followed its surrender. Here the sheriffdoms of Yorkshire and Lincoln, with the castles of York and Scarborough, had been put up for sale. A second coronation was to occur at Easter, and William thought it a favorable time to present his claims. The kings met at Clipston, near the Sherwood forests. William asked to have the provisions for his entertainment in coming to the English court fufilled, and also demanded that Northumberland, Cumberland, Westmoreland, and the honor of Lancaster should be restored to him "de jure praedecessorum suorum." Richard promised to consult his barons in a council at Northampton. They advised him that he ought not to make these concessions, as the princes of France, who were nearly all hostile to him, would attribute it to fear rather than love. As an offset to this, however, he confirmed by a special charter the dignities and honors promised to the king of Scotland.[2] Hoveden, who gives

Efforts to Regain the Northern Counties

---

[1] Chron. Melrose, and Hailes' Annals, I, p. 148; Bain, Cal. Docts., Nos. 199, 202, 205, 214, 224. This sum may have been the feudal aid for ransoming the lord of his fiefs, though from the later history it appears more like a gift to gain Richard's good will in regard to the northern counties. Earl David was freed by the king of the scutage for his ransom. (Bain, Cal. Docts., I, Nos. 221, 237 ; Early Kings, I, p. 397; Hoveden, An. 1194.)

[2] Letter regarding the fee given to the king of Scotland in his journey, and for the liberations to him to be doubled and allocated during his stay in the K.'s court :

Richard K. of England has given and confirmed to William K. of Scotland his friend and cousin and liegeman, and his heirs forever, all the liberties and rights which his ancestors were wont to have coming to the English court, remaining there, and returning therefrom ; namely, each day after crossing the marches of England on the K.'s mandate, 100s. sterling, and as much on his return until he reaches his own land ; and on each day during his stay at court 30s. sterling; and 12 of the K.'s

the substance of this charter in his own language, says that whenever the king of Scots came to court on the summons of the king of England, he was to be received "ad aquam de Tuede" by the bishop of Durham and the sheriff of Northumberland, and brought in safety to the Tees, and so on to the south. In returning also, he was to be conducted by the respective bishops and sheriffs "donec pervenerit ad aquam de Tuede." As the Tees marked the north boundary of York, so the Tweed set the limit to Northumberland and the northern extent of the kingdom of England.

In token of friendship, and as the representative of his English fiefs, William participated in Richard's second coronation at Winchester, carrying, as Earl David had formerly done, one of the swords of state. Perhaps he still hoped to win a larger part of his claims, for when Hugh, bishop of Durham, gave up the county of Northumberland, William at once offered 15,000 marks for it and its appurtenances. The offer was a tempting one to Richard, but he would not include the castles and without the political advantages they would afford William cared little for the pecuniary value of the fief. A few days later another attempt was made, but, says Hoveden, "It was not a

domain wastels (dominis guastellis); and a like number of simnells of same; and 12 sesterces of wine, viz., 4 of the K.'s domain wine, with which he is served, and 8 . . . . ; and 2 stones of wax, or 4 candles; and 40 of the domain candles, with which the K. of England is served; and 80 candles of the kind served to the K.'s house; and 2 pounds of pepper; and 4 pounds of cinnamon (cimini); and besides, the attendance which his ancestors had coming to and returning from the court of England, viz., that the Bishop of Durham, and the sheriff and barons of Northumberland, shall receive him on the marches and conduct him to the Tees; and there the Archbishop of York, and the sheriff and barons of that shire shall receive and conduct him to the bishopric of Lincoln; where the Bishop of Lincoln and sheriffs and barons of the county shall receive and conduct him through their bailliaries; and in like manner the bishops and sheriffs of the provinces through which he shall pass to Court. Wherefore the K. wills and firmly commands that K. William and his heirs shall have the aforesaids forever, both in expenses and conducts, and in fugitives who shall wish to defend themselves from felony at the English court, in peace; the bishops, sheriffs, and barons doing the said services, and keeping all other rights and liberties, and each sheriff finding the foresaid expenses in his bailliary.

Witnesses.—April 17, 1194.
Bain, I, No. 226; Foedera, I, p. 87.

part of the king's plan to deliver any castles to him; nevertheless he gave him hope of having them in future, after his return from Normandy." The next day William returned disappointed to Scotland, and the kings never met again.[1]

The following year William fell ill at Clackmannan, and assembled his barons to consider the question of the succession. He wished to settle it on Otho, son of Henry, duke of Saxony, and nephew of Richard, on condition that Otho should marry his eldest daughter, Margaret. A strong party, headed by Earl Patrick of Dunbar, opposed this, on the ground that it was not the custom that a woman should possess the kingdom, so long as a nephew or brother of her race survived who might possess it. William's speedy recovery did not lead to a change of mind, and the next year a conference on the subject was held at York with Hubert, archbishop of Canterbury, justiciar of England, and legate of the Apostolic See. Margaret was to have Lothian as her dowry, while all Northumberland and the county of Carlisle were to be given to the royal pair by Richard. Lothian, with its castles, was to be held by Richard, Northumberland and Carlisle, with their castles, by William. Had Lothian been an English fief, it would have been little to Richard's satisfaction to gain the custody of his own earldom in exchange for all Northumberland and the county of Carlisle. Lothian evidently was not a part of Northumberland at this time, nor did it sustain any feudal relation to England. Hopes of an heir led William to delay the execution of this plan, and in 1190 a son was born, Alexander II, to whom, at the age of three years, the barons of the realm swore fealty. Richard had died in 1199, and the clouds of doubt and strife which hung over England and Normandy on the accession of John began to darken the horizon of Scotland's future.[2]

[1] Hoveden, An. 1194.
[2] Hoveden, An. 1195; Hailes' Annals, I, p. 149; Early Kings, I, p. 399.

CHAPTER VI.

THE PERIOD OF THE GREAT CHARTER.

To interpret the events of this period aright, it is essential to recall the amalgamating forces which were drawing England and Scotland into closer relations. The marriage of Malcolm and Margaret was followed by that of Henry and "good Queen Maud." Her brother David, a welcome guest at Henry's court, married the widow of a rich, powerful English earl, and gathered about him that band of Norman nobility whose descendants were to claim the Scottish crown. It was part of a common policy now to push out the bounds of territory and dominion by the peaceful methods of marriage and inheritance, rather than by the conquests of war. The kingdom of England was dotted over with Scottish holdings. The Scottish descendants of Cospatric are now found as far south as Wiltshire. Alexander II holds lands in ten counties of England. Of the illegitimate daughters of William the Lion, Isabella married Robert de Brus, and later Robert de Ros; Ada married Earl Patrick of Dunbar; Margaret was married to Eustace de Vesci, and Aufrida to William de Say. Of his three daughters by Ermengarde, Margaret was married to Hubert de Burgh, the actual ruler of England during the minority of Henry III, Isabella to Roger Bigod, earl of Norfolk, and the beautiful Marjory—who was sought by Henry himself—was eventually wedded to Gilbert, the mareschal, earl of Pembroke. William's brother, David, lived to old age, leaving several children. His only surviving son, John "the Scot," inherited the earldoms of Chester and Lincoln through his mother, and the Huntingdon lands through his father. Of the daughters, Dervorguil gave the family of Balliol its claim to the Scottish crown, Ada married Henry de Hastings, and Isabella,

Anglo-Scotch Relations

the wife of Robert Bruce, became the mother of a noble line of kings. These are only a few illustrations of the way in which the two kingdoms were knit together by the bonds of family and feudal ties.[1] Hence, when the child-king of Scotland marries the little daughter of Henry III, it is not strange to find the father taking an active part in the regency, not as feudal lord of Scotland, but on the ground of consanguinity, while his letters under the royal seal disclaim any purpose to undermine the liberties or independence of the kingdom of Scotland. It was a favorite method of the times for a strong lord to grant a fief to a weaker one, in the hope of eventually finding a pretext for establishing a claim it was never intended to concede. And undoubtedly a part of the English claims on Scotland arose in this way. They came more largely, however, through the mingling of family and national relations than through a set purpose to unjustly extend the English power on the basis of the feudal relation.

A certain class of historians takes special pleasure in putting Scotland and Wales in the same category, as dependencies of England. But such a theory is quite untenable. The true relation between the Scottish and English kings was that which existed between the English kings and their French overlords. There was, however, this marked difference. A greater unity territorially, ethnically, and feudally existed at this period between the northern and southern kingdoms of Britain than between England and France — a unity which resulted in the severance of England from her continental possessions, and joined her with the independent kingdom of Scotland. The *independence of the kingdom* was steadily guarded by the men of Scotland as a precious treasure. It was acknowledged by the kings of England, and, except during the reign of Henry II, was

---

[1] Bain, Cal. Docts., I, Nos. 5, 10, 12, 686. On genealogy *cf*. Hailes' Annals, and Early Kings. Duncan, Earl of Fife, pays 500 marks for the custody of Roger de Merlay's land and his son, in Northumberland, "and that the son may marry the said earl's daughter." For a fine of £200 Alexander II has the ward and marriage of the heirs of David de Lindesi, with custody of their lands in *eleven* counties of England. (Bain, I, Nos. 191, 822-3.)

never lost till the direct line of Scottish kings became extinct, and their descendants, through the related Anglo-Norman stock, submitted their claims to the great Edward. Even then the true Scot spirit revealed itself. "According as they [the competitors for the crown of Scotland] supported or withstood the rights of their own prince [Edward of England] over the kingdom which they claimed," says Mr. Freeman, "some of them have won the name of Scottish traitors and others the name of Scottish patriots." He asserts that from 924–1328 "the vassalage of Scotland was an essential part of the public law of the isle of Britain;" and that "nothing is clearer than that this homage (1072) was paid, not only for Cumberland or Lothian, but for the true kingdom of the Celtic Picts and Scots." He then constructs an ingenious theory according to which this policy was carried out. The king of Scots held of the English king by three forms of tenure. He held his true kingdom north of the Forth and Clyde under a merely external supremacy; Scottish Cumbria as a territorial fief, and Lothian as an English earldom. The first objection to this view is that it presupposes a continuous feudal system in England from 924 to 1328—a view for which few advocates, if any, can be found. It would certainly be unjust to establish a true feudal claim on a non-feudal precedent. A second objection is that the facts regarding Scottish Cumbria and Lothian do not warrant such a theory. Nor, third, do they warrant a merely external supremacy over the kingdom north of the Forth and Clyde. For Richard released William the Lion from *all* homage and allegiance for the kingdom of Scotland. Such a supremacy, which brought with it absolutely no rights or privileges, no tribute or service, no power of interference unless gained in battle by the fate of arms, is at best an exceedingly hazy thing. In reality, it did not exist. Any such *appearance* is easily explicable through the peculiar feudal and family ties which were formed. The *fact* of such supremacy is disproved by the best sources. The only basis for such a conception lies in the mythical "commendation" of 924, —truly a slender foundation on which to rear the massive feudal structure of later ages. From David to Alexander III Scottish kings were, indeed, vassals of an English overlord. But the relation was a purely personal one, and homage was rendered only for English fiefs. It never embraced the kingdom of Scotland, except when extorted as the ransom of a captive king.[1]

The accession of John brought little joy to either England or Scotland. He had many attractive personal graces, and considerable gifts as a politician, diplomat, and warrior. But morally he was rotten to the core. "In his inner soul John was the worst outcome of the Angevins. He united into one mass of wickedness their insolence, their selfishness, their unbridled lust, their cruelty and tyranny, their shamelessness, their superstition, their cynical indifference to honor or truth."[2] On the death of Richard, John at once sent his representatives to England to receive oaths of fealty from his subjects. In a meeting at Northampton they pledged their word to David, the brother of the king of Scots, and many others of the barons whose support was doubtful, that John would give to each of them full justice if they would preserve their fealty to him. King William sent messengers from the north, demanding a restoration of his patrimony. But the English officials would not permit them to cross over to Normandy, sending Earl David instead to William, to urge him patiently to wait for John's arrival in England. John also sent a message to William by Eustace de Vesci, promising him full satisfaction of his demands if he would meanwhile keep the peace. In May, 1199, the king landed in England and was crowned at Westminster. Roger, bishop of St. Andrews, was present at the coronation, apparently to look out for the interests of the Scottish king, but there is no mention of Earl David. Soon after, John gave a hearing to William's messengers, but evaded giving an answer to their demands for the northern counties, and again sought a meeting with William, hoping he would come to him at Nottingham. The king of Scots refused to appear, and threatened war

King John

[1] Freeman, Wm. Rufus, II, p. 126; Norman Conq., I, pp. 59, 124.
[2] Green, Hist. Eng., I, p. 229.

if his claims were not conceded. John was ready neither to yield nor to fight, and evaded a final answer by placing the disputed territory under the care of a powerful baron, while he hastened over sea. Seeing that his efforts for a settlement were in vain, the king of the Scots collected forces to carry out his threat of war. But doubt and fear oppressed him. His kingdom had suffered much from the folly of his youth. Age and sickness were breaking down his spirit. His heir was hardly out of the cradle, and not yet established as his successor. Seeking for guidance, he spent the night before the shrine of St. Margaret, at Dunfermline. To his troubled mind, a divine admonition seemed to warn him against attempting to secure his rights by force. He accordingly disbanded his army.[1]

John meanwhile had plunged into war with Philip II. Normandy and Aquitaine had submitted to him, but Anjou declared for Arthur. Philip supported the Angevins, but alienated them by retaining the castles he took. This led to a truce between the kings, during which John returned to England. Hoping to meet the king of Scots, he came to York, but was again disappointed, and returned to Normandy. In May he met Philip, who restored to him Evreux and all the conquests he had made in Normandy. John, however, became the "man" of Philip, and conferred all he had just received on Philip's son Louis, as his bride's marriage dower. Having thus been recognized by his feudal lord as Richard's heir, he again crossed the channel with his new wife, Isabella of Angoulême, and was recrowned with her at Westminster. He now sent a distinguished delegation, many of them related to the king of Scotland by marriage, "cum litteris regiis patentibus de salvo conducto," to bring about the long-deferred meeting. Earl David had been sent previously,

---

[1] Hoveden, An. 1199. The sensitiveness of the feudal relation between the two kingdoms at this time is well illustrated by an insignificant event. A flood carried away a bridge at Berwick-on-Tweed. The king of Scots ordered Earl Patrick "custos de Berwic," to rebuild it. But the bishop of Durham forbade him to sink a foundation for it on the lands of Durham. The bishop at length yielded the point, but it was "salva conventione" which had existed between the bishop's predecessor and the king of Scotland. So easy was it to establish a feudal claim without any basis of right.

It seems probable that William was unwilling to meet John until the latter had confirmed Richard's charter of dignities and liberties. Rumors of an alliance between the Scottish heir and a French princess at last caused John to hastily dispatch an honorable escort to the north with the desired charter. William's point was thus gained, and in November, 1200 A. D., the two kings met at Lincoln for the first time, to discuss the points at issue. The following day another conference was held on a high hill outside the city, and William there did homage to John in the sight of all the people.[1] It is noteworthy that there is no mention of any oaths of fealty on the part of William's barons, as under Henry II. The vague character of the homage, "de jure suo," with the reservation by William "salvo jure suo," was evidently part of an agreement with John that after homage had been rendered the Scottish claims should receive consideration and settlement. For the king of Scotland at once demands "totam Northumbriam, Cumbriam, et Westmerilande, sicut jus et haereditatem." The subject was discussed, but no settlement was reached, and John asked time for consideration. It was granted, and the king of Scotland returned home. The treacherous John then asked for further delay and crossed over to Normandy. What the final outcome was is unknown, for with the close of Hoveden's narrative all reference to the subject ceases. The lack of a northern chronicler, as Mr. Robertson remarks, is deeply felt. The monk of St. Albans who succeeds Hoveden does not hesitate to omit "salvo jure suo" from the MS. he copies, when it guards the independence of the northern kingdom.[2]

John's base conduct in securing Isabella as his wife roused the barons of Poitou to take up arms. He appealed them for

[1] Hoveden, An. 1200; Early Kings, I, p. 417, note; Bain, Cal. Docts., Nos. 299, 292, 371, 389, 396; Hailes' Annals, I, p. 151. William "devenit homo J. regis Angliae de jure suo et juravit ei fidelitatem . . . . de vita et membris et terreno honore suo, contra omnes homines et de pace servanda sibi et regno suo, *salvo jure suo*."

[2] It is important to remember the feudal custom was *homage* first, then settlement of fiefs. (Hoveden, An. 1201; Wendover, 1200; Early Kings, I, p. 418; II, p. 414, and often, on Lingard's gross inaccuracies.)

treason, but they refused to accept his wager of battle and turned to Philip, who in 1202 summoned John to answer their complaints before his peers. John refused to respond and was declared forfeited of all lands which he held as Philip's vassal. His wickedness and tyranny, the death of Arthur, and the growth of a national spirit among the French, made Philip's conquest of Normandy, Maine, Anjou, Touraine, and part of Poitou, an easy matter.

The death of Hubert Walter, archbishop of Canterbury, in 1205, also involved John in conflict with the church, and in 1209 he was formally excommunicated by Innocent III. During this period the relations between the kings of England and Scotland, though not hostile, were far from cordial, and William's devotion to the see of Rome, after the interdict, was rewarded by a papal bull, which confirmed him in "every liberty and immunity that had at any time been conferred upon the king, church, or kingdom of Scotland." But there had been no absolute break with John. A letter of July 24, 1205, illustrates the diplomatic negotiations which were being carried on, some of which were kept secret:

The King to the King of Scotland. Thanks him much for the messengers whom he sent, and the good answer he gives regarding the business between them, which he hopes, 'Deo Volente' may be perfected. Informs him that the messengers are retained for the present, as he is to hold a council of his bishops and barons at the feast of the Blessed Peter 'ad vincula,' on account of the death of H[ubert] Archbishop of Canterbury. He also awaits an answer from R[oger] constable of Chester, and others whom he had sent to the Scottish king. And after taking advice of the Council thereon, and getting meanwhile an answer from his said messengers, he will hasten to meet William, as he shall hear from them, to finish the above business, or do better as God shall teach him, as to the matters pending between them. Assures William he is well pleased with the exception made in his letter regarding the land of Tundale [Tynedale] to be retained by him, of which no mention was made in the agreement discussed between them, as he [William] was previously seized of it. Has done all in good faith.[1]

[1] Bain, Cal. Docts., I, No. 368.

On November 30, of the same year, a safe-conduct was issued, with the usual escort, for a meeting at York in the following February. It grants William

.... if by chance, 'quod absit,' he (John) withdraws by evil or otherwise, a forty days' truce before returning to his land, so that in the interim there may be no forfeiture by John or his men, to William, his land or men; sends him Earl David his brother, to remain in Scotland till his return, as he asked of John by his messengers.[1]

This entry illustrates the scrupulous care necessary to guard against John's duplicity, and also the fact that the possible forfeiture of the English fiefs held by the king of Scotland and his barons was a matter of the greatest moment. It was not the fiefs only, important as they were, but also the possible right of succession to the English crown which they carried with them, that so often influenced the policy of the Scottish kings. They preferred to make every concession, save the independence of the kingdom, rather than imperil their possessions and claims by an appeal to the sword. It was this policy which raised up among their own subjects a hostile party, which threatened to subvert the kingdom.

Another safe-conduct was issued " for coming to treat with " John, in March, 1206-7, and the last of June, 1207, the sheriff of York is allowed " 10l. for the expenses of the K. of Scots, for the first year, and 15l. in this year, when he (John) was last at York." Robert fitz Roger is allowed 30l., "which he laid out for the expenses of the K. of Scots, when he came to the K. at York, by the K.'s precept." Again in October, 1207, the process is repeated for a meeting "at Martinmas next" at York, William "to stay there to speak with him [John] and to return to his own country." Allowances for expenses are made, as usual, from Yorkshire (15l.) and Northumberland (30l.). How much light might be thrown on disputed points could the tenor of these private meetings and compacts be known! The above entries show the barrenness of the English chronicles—which record no meetings of the kings between 1200

---

[1] Bain., I, No. 368.

and 1209 — and confirm the accounts of the Scottish writers.[1]

In the meantime England and Wales were suffering the penalties of the interdict, which only served apparently to increase John's tyranny and cruelty. His subjects "began seriously to consider what prince there was in whose bosom they might find a refuge." The sentence of excommunication hung over the king's head, and began to be whispered through the streets. His efforts to build a castle at Tweedmouth, threatening the growing interests of Berwick, had also aroused warm feeling in the north. According to Fordun, the work, begun some years previously, had been leveled with the ground by the Scots, as often as the English attempted its erection. A stormy meeting of the kings in 1204 had been without definite results. Now, another foreign alliance was set on foot, which probably contemplated the union of the prince of Scotland with the heiress of Hainault and Flanders — a project which would receive the hearty support of Philip. As lord of William's English fiefs, John had a right to a voice in the marriage of his children, and the transmission of those fiefs.[2] The fort at Tweedmouth had been razed, too, and any foreign alliance was looked on with the suspicion of disloyalty. For these reasons John prepared to hasten north with a large army. The king of Scotland, posted at Roxburgh, was summoned to meet him at Newcastle. His illness, however, delayed negotiations, and his final answer, prompted perhaps by the war party in Scotland, roused John's wrath. The king of England had already expressed joy at William's recovery, and

. . . . comes to meet him at . . . . to confer with him and settle matters long discussed between them.

Now, he threatens war. But the interests which bound the

---

[1] Fordun grows more reliable as he approaches his own era. On the errors of Wendover *cf.* Early Kings, I, p. 423, note; Bain, I Nos. 389, 396, 399, 401, 403, 410, 417, 422.

[2] This shows the *personal* feudal relation between the kings and their families stretched to its fullest extent.

men of the two kingdoms to a peace policy prevailed, and William met the king of England at Norham (Northampton— Foedera) to treat for peace. Terms were agreed upon in August, 1209. William promised 15,000 marks, in four payments, " for having the good will of his said lord the K. of England, and fulfilling the conventions between them, confirmed on either side by charters." For securing payment of which sums

.... et ad praedictos terminos reddenda, et pro eisdem terminis fideliter tenendis, dedimus ei in tenentiam, obsides nostros quos habet, et qui in praedictis Cartis nostris nominati sunt ; exceptis duabis filiabus nostris quas ei liberavimus. Et cum praedictam pecuniam .... ei persolverimus, ipse nobis hanc Cartam nostram reddet quietam.

The omission of the names of William's daughters from the list of hostages in the Close Rolls, and the exception made above, intimate that the chroniclers are in error in regarding them as hostages. They were sent to England to be married, and remained there after John's death, though the hostages were restored. In 1211-12 the bishopric of Durham reports a writ of 4l. 6s. " for carriage of 7,000 marks of the K. of Scotland's fine from Norham to Nottingham." The Foedera contains " Duae Cedulae " of all the bulls, charters, and other muniments in the king of Scotland's treasury at Edinburgh, inspected in 1282, on the order of Alexander III, by three of his clerks. Among the " Negotia tangentia Angliam " the following occurs : "Item, Litera Reg. Johannis, ad recipiendum septem mil. et. D. Marc. ad opus Reg. Angliae pro quodam fine, et de residuo remittendo." This corroborates the testimony of the Exchequer records, which make no mention of any further payment. Another entry : " Item, Litera R. Johannis quod non possit Castrum firmari super portum de Twedmuth," throws light on John's part in the treaty, and shows that William maintained the stand he had taken against the erection of an English fortress at Tweedmouth.[1]

[1] Fordun, Annals, § XXV ; Early Kings, I, pp. 418-20 ; II, p. 414 ; Mt. West., Triveti, Hemingburgh, An. 1209 ; Bain, Cal. Docts., I, Nos. 450-93 ; Foedera, I, pp. 215-16.

Having also secured himself against the forfeiture of his feifs and rights in England, he was now at liberty to turn against those of his own subjects who got nothing out of the English alliance, and for that reason, or on general principles, opposed it.[1] John also had pressing demands calling him to the south. In this year he received the homage of the free tenants of his realm, and compelled the Welsh nobles to come to Woodstock to perform the same duty. Had Scotland been a dependent kingdom, her nobles would have received a similar summons as they did under Henry II. The rebellious elements in both kingdoms drew the kings into closer alliance, in order to secure the succession of their young sons. They met at Durham, and subsequently at Norham, the queen of Scotland also using her influence to secure favorable terms. It seems probable that both kings agreed, in case of the death of one, that the survivor should support the rightful heir to the throne. William also granted to John the marriage of his son Alexander, as his liegeman,[2] within six years from date, "so that it be without disparagement," and both father and son promised to be faithful to John's son Henry as their liege lord, and to maintain him in his kingdom with all their power. Alexander was knighted soon after by the English king, in London. This arrangement left John free from any fears regarding a foreign alliance with Scotland, and William could devote his failing energies to putting down the rebellious element in his own kingdom.[3]

[1] It may be asked why the English kings kept up an arrangement to the apparent advantage of the king of Scots. It was (1) a convenient means of securing peace on the border; (2) the inevitable outcome of the relations thus established. Claims were originated which were sure of a marvelous development. (3) An effort to realize the elusive dream of becoming overlord in the kingdom of Scotland, or of uniting the two kingdoms by marriage. The effort for a legislative and commercial union of two independent kingdoms finds its opportunity and begins to take form under Edward I, but is foiled by the death of the Maid of Norway.

[2] Alexander seems to have met John at Alnwick in 1210, where he did homage "pro omnibus rectitudinibus." Payment of the balance of the 15,000 marks may have been remitted here. (Early Kings, I, p. 424.)

[3] Mt. Paris, Hist. Ang., p. 119; Fordun Annals, § XXVI; Bain, Cal. Docts., I, Nos. 501, 508, 518, 522; Wendover, An. 1212; Early Kings, I, pp. 424, 428.

Events in England were hastening the advent of Magna Charta. According to Hemingburgh, the revolt of the barons was precipitated in part by the lust of their king. In 1212 he mustered his forces to repress a fierce rising headed by Llewellyn of Wales. While at Nottingham he received messages from his natural daughter, Joanna, wife of Llewellyn, and from the king of Scotland, that his life was not safe if he ventured into the mountain fastnesses of Wales. He put more faith in these warnings because, by his excommunication, his subjects had been absolved from their allegiance to him. He, therefore, disbanded his army, and returning to London demanded hostages from all his suspected nobles. Robert fitz Walter and Eustace de Vesci were so deeply implicated that they fled—the former to France, the latter to his father-in-law, the king of Scotland. For De Vesci had married his natural daughter, Margaret. John, attracted by her beauty, had sought her out, only to be repulsed. His anger was visited on De Vesci, who may have planned to wipe out the insult by the death of the depraved king. Thus the conspiracy arose, and it was, perhaps, through his daughter that William got the information he laid before John. The flight of the latter's vassal to the north brought him again to the frontier, but the illness of William prevented a meeting. John urged that Alexander be sent in his father's stead. Though he offered magnificent inducements, the majority of the Scottish council feared his duplicity, and declared that Alexander, who might be retained as security for De Vesci, should not leave the kingdom. John was, therefore, compelled to return to the south without accomplishing his object.[1]

After a reign of almost fifty years, William the Lion passed away amid the beautiful surroundings of Stirling castle (December 4, 1214). During his life he maintained the same general relations with John as with Richard. The legal processes of the day are suggested by pleas—in which Earl David appears—of novel disseizin, concerning boundaries, etc., some

---

[1] Heming. Chron., An. 1215; Wendover, An. 1212; Early Kings, I, pp. 430-1; Fordun, Annals, § XXVII.

of which stand over *sine die*, "as the earl is in the K.'s service beyond sea," or "has gone to Scotland by the K.'s precept,"
and shall meanwhile "have peace from all imparlances summonses and demands." The position of the king of Scotland as tenant-in-chief of the lands subinfeoffed to his brother is clearly shown. A certain Wido sought a warrandice from Earl David "of the land of which he had a charter" from the earl's grandfather. David's attorney

<small>General Relations between John and William</small>

.... came and said that the Earl was not the heir of Earl David, his grandfather. For the K. of Scotland holds that heritage, of whom the Earl himself holds. The Earl has not taken the homage of Wido. The court decides he is not bound to warrant.

But David also held lands directly of the king of England, as illustrated by John's grant to him of the manor of Totham, "to be held by two knights' service," and of "all Gumecester, and 25 marks of land in Nasinton and Jarewelle for the service of one knight, as in the charters of his brother Richard." It is this double form of tenure which occasions, and at the same time explains, the homages of the King of Scotland and of his sons or men who hold lands in England, either under him or directly of the English king. Such barons were placed in an unpleasant predicament in the event of war, nor was it easy to avoid conflict in time of peace. A good illustration is the case of Ranulf de Bonekil, a well-known border chief, who

.... on account of the service of his lord the K. of Scotland, could not attend the recognizance of great assize. .... He is not to be put in default, or lose anything by absence, as the K. has guaranteed him that day. The sheriff is also to accept his attorney to follow the county and pleas, and do suit and service for his land. The K. has granted this, for the love & at the request of Alexander, son of the K. of Scots.[1]

The court records afford many examples of this double tenure, as well as many other interesting details — some of which ought to be noted. In Northampton "Earl David owes 50 marks

[1] Bain, Cal. Docts., I, Nos. 269-71, 274, 290, 310, 542, 693.

for the ward of the land and the heir of Stephen de Cameis." In Cambridge and Huntingdon he owes 1,000 marks "that Henry his son[1] may have to wife Matilda de Calceto (Cauz) with her land." As Henry failed to get the lady the fine was remitted, and the rich heiress of Ralf de Cornhille was given him instead, "with the land pertaining to her."

The expansion of commerce appears in a number of interesting entries, showing the relations of the two kingdoms. Frequent mention is made of scutage, sometimes due, often discharged to Earl David. William de Breosa "gives ten bulls and ten cows not to go to Scotland to attend the K. of Scotland to the K." Aaron, a famous Jew of Lincoln, passes into history as the creditor of the king of Scotland to the amount of 2,776l., for which Earl David became surety.[2]

One of the most striking illustrations of the complicated nature of the feudal relation at this period is the case of Alan and Thomas, of Galloway. This district was exceedingly restive under Scottish overlordship. Malcolm IV repressed this spirit, but after the capture of William the Lion the turbulence of the lords of Galloway became more marked than ever. In accordance with the terms made at Falaise they, with the other Scottish barons, swore fealty to Henry II. Though lawfully still subject to the king of Scots, they sought, and seem in one case to have obtained, the right of direct dependence upon the crown of England, even for their lands in Galloway. This was a distinct infringement of William's rights, as set forth in the articles of Falaise, but he seems to have acquiesced in the usurpation, either because he did not feel strong enough to resent it by force, or because it was arranged in some of the secret treaties between himself and John. A charter of John's (July 8, 1212)

. . . . grants to Edgar son of Dovenald the reasonable gift made by Henry the K.'s father, of his own land, and all the land which Ewarn

---

[1] Henry of Brechin, a natural son. (Bain, I, Nos. 281, 334, 350, 365.)

[2] Bain, I, Nos. 273, 558; 331, 363, 452, 599, 600; 282, 375, 433, 457, 484, 490.

his brother held in Straddune of the K. of Scotland, the day he died. To be held in fee as in Henry's charter.

The same day the king received the homage of Edgar and his son Fergus, and took "themselves, their men, their lands, tenures, and possessions, into his protection; and warrants them as his own domains against all injuries." And under the same date is an entry "for the expenses of Edgar de Gaweia (of Galloway), who came to the K. with twenty horses and twenty men, for four days." Mr. Bain says these charters "are remarkable as evidence of the claim of superiority over Cumbria, for the name of the land, 'Straddune,' indicates a site north of the Solway." But the inference does not seem well taken. For, while the land very possibly lay north of the Solway, there is every evidence that the king of England was acting beyond his rights in making grants there, availing himself of the conditions which arose after the capture of the Scottish king and of the hostility which the Galwegians felt to their natural and customary overlord. The charters are rather against the claim to superiority in Scottish Cumbria than otherwise. John speaks of the *reasonable* gift—an expression not met with elsewhere. He takes Edgar and his son Fergus, "their men, their lands, tenures, and possessions, *into his protection;*" he warrants them "*as his own domains*, against *all injuries*." These expressions, when viewed in the light of Galloway's previous hostility to the kings of Scotland and her punishment for the same, seem to indicate an unjustifiable action on John's part and a fear of Scottish reprisals on the part of his vassals. In any case, there is no evidence that this condition existed till after the capture of the Scottish king, nor was the usurpation based on any precedent claim of superiority over this region. There is no doubt that Galloway, as a whole, remained under the independent control of the kings of Scotland, except during the later years of Henry II. The fact that this grant of lands north of the Solway is the only instance of its kind, invites the query whether after all "Straddune" was not south of the Solway, among the English fiefs of the Scottish king, or among the "debatable lands" on the western border, which continued to be a refuge for outlaws and criminals as late as the union of the two kingdoms, in 1707.[1]

Thomas and Alan of Galloway held extensive fiefs in England. From Worcestershire account is rendered against Thomas of "1000 marks for having the land which was Hugh de Say's." From Warwickshire he makes return for "two knights and four parts." He had large holdings in Ireland, besides his earldom of Athol in Scotland. Alan occupied a still more prominent place. He was the son of Roland, already mentioned, who, though he did homage to Henry II with the Scottish barons, remained a loyal vassal of William the Lion, apparently marrying into the royal family. Alan succeeded his father in the high office of constable of Scotland. His wife was the eldest daughter of Earl David and the earl of Chester's sister. He was also related to King John, who conferred on him large estates in Ireland. Through his mother, Helena, a daughter of Richard de Moreville, he inherited English fiefs in the shires of Northampton and Rutland. Hence it is not strange to find him assisting John in his wars in Wales. There is no evidence, however, that either he or Thomas were anything but loyal vassals of William the Lion for their possessions in Scotland and Galloway.[2]

---

[1] *Cf.* Enc. Brit. on Cumberland; Bain, Cal. Docts., I, Introd., p. xxxii, Nos. 523, 525-6.

[2] Bain, Cal. Docts., I, Nos. 426, 500, 513, 519, 531, 550, 553, 560, 573, 580, 583-6. July 20, 1212: The K. to his faithful cousin Alan de Galweia. "Requests him for the great business regarding which he lately asked him, and as he loves him, to send him 1000 of his best and most active Galwegians so as to be at Chester on Sunday next after the assumption of the Blessed Mary instant. And if he can send them at his own cost, it will greatly please the K.; but if not, he is to send them to Carlisle, where the K. will provide their pay; and Alan is to place over them a constable, who knows how to keep peace in the K.'s army and harass his enemies." In August he receives 300 marks "by way of gift," "to pay his squires who had come with him in the K.'s service for the army of Wales." Had Galloway been a dependency of the English crown, Alan would have been *summoned* as any other English baron. The King, however, begs a favor of him, on the plea of kinship and his great need, and of the favors Alan had received at his hands. He promises to pay the men if necessary, and eventually does so. This rather contravenes the evidence for the claim of superiority over Cumbria, and makes it necessary to explain the grant of Straddune on some other basis. (Bain, I, Nos. 529, 533.)

The apparently dry Exchequer Records afford an interesting glimpse of the social life of the thirteenth century, in accounting for the expenses of the Scottish princesses committed to John's care. Geoffrey fitz Piers "owes ten palfreys and ten goshawks, that the K. of Scotland's daughters may not be committed to him in ward." He is pardoned the palfreys, and only the goshawks may be demanded. Their journey from Bristol to Nottingham is accompanied by the convoy of 48,000 marks from the Bristol treasury. 36*l*. 18*s*. 4*d*. are expended "for the robes of the K. of Scotland's daughters and their governesses" (magistrarum). At Windsor two seams (summae) of fish, fifty pounds of almonds (amigdalarum), and one hundred pounds of figs (figis) are bought for their use. At Nottingham they have robes of green, trimmed with rabbits' fur, and russet hoods. There is also a russet rain-hood (capa pluvialis) for the use of their master. Their father sends the royal falconers with a gift of girfalcons to the king, and Adam de la Mark receives 20s. by way of gift, for carrying a like present from John to the king of Scotland. In May, 1213, the princesses are "at the house of the Temple, near Dover." The last of June they are at Corfe, and the king commands the mayor and reeves of Winchester to provide for the queen, his niece [Eleanor of Brittany], and the two daughters of the king of Scotland, "robes and hoods, and other necessary clothes." In July the mayor is to send "in haste" robes of dark green, and for the use of the three maids robes of bright green, a hood for rainy weather, cloaks furred with lambskin, thin summer shoes (stivalia), and a saddle with gilded reins for the king's niece. But back of all this there lay a distinct political purpose. There is little doubt that John intended, contrary to his agreements, to retain the princesses in his charge, unmarried, in order that, should anything befall the sole male heir of William the Lion, he might marry his son Henry to one of William's daughters, and thus place the crowns of England and Scotland upon the head of his own heir.[1]

[1] Bain, Cal. Docts., I, Nos. 463, 530, 544, 559, 562–4, 572, 579, 581; Early Kings, I, p. 423, note.

The death of William the Lion left his son, Alexander II, a boy of sixteen years, as king of Scotland at a very critical period in the history of English liberties. As John remained obdurate, the pope had declared his deposition, and transferred his crown to the king of France. This agreed perfectly with the schemes of Philip Augustus, and he at once gathered an army to enforce the papal decree. John also summoned his barons to oppose Philip's landing. But he knew how bitterly many of them hated him. He had already been warned of the intrigues against his life. It was apparently the revelation of this conspiracy at home which now led him to suddenly yield all the papal demands. The exiled clergy were recalled, before whom the king made abject submission. Homage for England and Ireland, and an annual tribute of 1,000 marks, stamped him as the vassal of the pope. The statement that England "thrilled with a sense of shame" is perhaps too strong. The chonicles only faintly suggest such an idea. It is certain, however, that John went to the extreme limit in his subjection to the papal see. Even the imperious demands of Gregory VII had failed to win any such concession from Henry IV. But as a political move the act was worthy of the king's wily diplomacy. It rendered the preparations of his enemies useless. It brought the censure of the pope upon the barons who resisted the demand for service across the sea. It added the hearty support of Rome to that of John's sister's son, the Emperor Otto IV, and resulted in a joint attack on Philip. But the defeat of the imperial forces at Bouvines[1] compelled John to a truce without having regained anything north of the Loire, and turned the tide of events in favor of English freedom.

Alexander II, 1214–1249

In the struggle between the king and his barons, Earl David, now an aged man, had not escaped the suspicion of John. A curt dispatch of August 21, 1212, commands him to immediately deliver up the castle of Fotheringeia for the king's use. His son is held as a hostage for his fidelity. In October, however, he is again in the king's service, and in June, 1213, has the ward

[1] 1214 A. D. (Wendover, Ad. an.)

of a son of David de Lindescie, a hostage of the king. But in July or August of the following year Peter, bishop of Winchester writes that he

.... has much to discuss with him regarding the affairs of the K. and his kingdom, and directs him, as he loves the K.'s honour, and himself, and his hostages, and whatever he holds of the K., to put aside all delay and hindrance, and come to the parts of London, where he shall hear the writer is, ... to discuss said matters.

A little later the king commands the sheriffs of Cambridge and Huntingdon shires

.... to give to his beloved and faithful Earl David, his third penny in these counties, as he used to have.

And an order from Runnymede, June 21, 1215, restores his hostages and the castle of Foderingeya to him, as he "is to perform homage to the K."[1]

On the death of William the Lion, Alexander had been at once crowned king of Scotland at Scone. Though he sympathized with the English barons and had from them a promise of the northern counties in return for his co-operation, he took no active part, and in July, 1215, sent messengers to John "regarding his affairs at the English court." But after the king had repudiated his oath to the barons at Runnymede, Alexander crossed the border with his men and allied himself definitely with the king's enemies. The northern counties were made over to him as promised,[2] and the barons of Northumberland and Yorkshire, having first destroyed the means of subsistence, retired with the Scottish forces across the border and tendered their allegiance to the king of Scots. John set out for the north with his Flemings and Brabanters, and ravaged the country as far as Haddington, but was forced to retire for want of supplies. The Scots retaliated by ravages in Cumberland.[3]

---

[1] Bain, Cal. Docts., I, Nos. 534, 539, 541, 574, 601, 616, 622-3.

[2] The staff used by De Vesci in the ceremony was subsequently carried off by Edward I. *Cf.* Early Kings, II, pp. 4-5, note.

[3] Fordun, Annals, §§ 29, 33, 34; Mt. Paris, Chron. Maj., II, p. 641; Bain, I, No. 629; Foedera, I, p. 203.

The reversal of the pope's attitude toward John and his barons in the contest for their liberties, and the insufferable insolence and cruelty of the king, resulted in an appeal to France. Philip's eldest son Louis had a *quasi* claim to the throne through his wife, Blanche of Castile, who was a grand-daughter of Henry II. To the papal opposition Philip replied that the king of England had no right to transfer his kingdom to another without the consent of his barons. The ambition of Blanche urged her husband to action, and in May, 1216, he landed on the island of Thanet. Alexander again crossed the northern border, and marched triumphantly throughout the length of England to Dover, where he met Louis and did homage to him "de jure suo, quod de rege Anglorum tenere debuit." John meanwhile, wrathful but impotent, was planning to intercept and cut off the Scottish forces on their return. But disaster overtook him while crossing the Wash, and his death followed soon after. It is said that his own camp was sacked by the very army he had schemed to destroy.[1]

[1] Fordun, Annals, § 35; Mt. Paris, Chron. Maj., II, pp. 666-7.

CHAPTER VII.

THE REIGN OF ALEXANDER II.

Henry III, 1216-1272

The guardianship of John's nine-year-old son, who was crowned in his father's stead, was at once assumed by William the Marshall, earl of Pembroke, and Gualo, the papal legate. Hubert de Burgh also remained loyal, refusing to surrender the castle of Dover to Louis. The national spirit was growing, and men hoped for better things from Henry than they had received from John. Hence, Louis' cause steadily lost ground, and peace soon followed the battle of Lincoln (1217). Alexander's kingdom was placed under an interdict because he allied himself with the enemies of John, and refused to surrender the castle of Carlisle, which he had taken, to Henry. But a milder policy prevailed under Honorius III. In his first year he wrote a fatherly letter to Alexander, urging him to give up the alliance with Louis, and to renew his fealty to the king of England. He promised him the especial grace and favor of the Apostolic See, "and moreover to aid him in recovering Henry's favor, and also his own right." The treaty between Henry and Louis admitted Alexander to its terms, on condition of restoring the castle of Carlisle, and a reconciliation was soon brought about. At the same time Alexander was released from the interdict, though the craft of Gualo is said to have withheld a like favor from the people and clergy of Scotland, until they had "slaked the thirst of his money bag with draughts of money."[1]

Alexander Makes Peace

Safe-conducts were issued in November, 1217, and the constable of Chester was ordered to meet Alexander at Berwick,

[1] Bain, Cal. Docts., I, Nos. 664, 668; Mt. Paris, Chron. Maj., Ad. an; Fordun, Annals, §§ 36, 37.

and escort him to Northampton, where he did homage, and was put in full possession of his fiefs. On December 19 Henry wrote to the sheriff of Lincoln, commanding him—as Alexander, king of Scotland, "has come to his allegiance (ad fidem et servicium) and has done to the K. what he ought to do [1]—to give the said K. seizin of his lands and tenements which Earl David *held of him* (de eo) in his bailliary of the honour of Huntingdon." (Similar writs were sent to the sheriffs of *nine* counties— Leicester, Cambridge and Huntingdon, Northampton, Rutland, Bedford and Buckingham, Essex and Middlesex.) This letter shows: (1) the *extent* of the English fiefs held by the king of Scotland; (2) the fact that the earl of Huntingdon held that honor and other lands of the king of Scotland as *tenant-in-capite;* (3) that these lands had been so held *before* the meeting at Northampton. The homage done for them previously was now repeated in token of peace and renewal of fealty.[2]

Two years later Alexander's uncle, David, died. One son, John "the Scot," survived him. The custody of the honor of Huntingdon, till the heir should come of age, was granted to Alexander as *tenant-in-capite*. About this time he set negotiations on foot to bring about the marriage of himself and his sisters. The limit of six years stipulated in the last agreement between his father and John had already expired, and nothing had been done. Alexander referred the matter to Honorius, who, in 1218, had confirmed in the strongest terms the liberties and independence of church, kingdom, and king of Scotland. Conferences were held at Norham between Alexander, Pandulph, the papal legate, and Stephen de Segrave, chief procurator for the king of England. An agreement was finally reached and arrangements made for a meeting of the kings at York in June, 1230. The earl of Warrenne conducted the royal

Death of Earl David

Marriage of Alexander

---

[1] A general term used with reference to any expression of homage or fealty. *Cf.* Bain, I, No. 743. The widow of Gerard de Furnevalle is commanded "to do to Alex., K. of Scotland, what she ought, for the lands held of him in England."

[2] Bain, I, Nos. 673, 678-9, 684, 686. On Lingard's statements *cf.* Early Kings, II, p. 8.

guest from Berwick bridge. There are the usual entries for the corrody of the king. Henry promised to give Alexander his eldest sister, Joanna, in marriage. If this could not be done,[1] he should have the younger sister, Isabella, within fifteen days of the ensuing feast of St. Michael. Margaret and Isabella, sisters of the king of Scotland, were to be honorably married within a year, *within the realm of England;*[2] or if not, they were to be returned safely within a month after the said term, to their own land. Alexander agreed to this arrangement, and documents properly witnessed were exchanged on both sides.[3]

The following May the king of Scotland was escorted with all the feudal honors and dignities of his forefathers from Berwick to the Tees by the archbishop of York, the earls and barons and sheriff of Northumberland, and the seneschal of the bishop of Durham, who was the king's chancellor; and from the Tees, by the sheriff and barons of York, to the capital of the north, where his marriage with Joanna was duly solemnized. At the same time his sister Margaret was wedded to Hubert de Burgh, the powerful justiciar and practical ruler of England.[4] So long as this man stood at the head of affairs, there was peace and justice between the two kingdoms. He represented the national spirit, and was intensely jealous of foreign control. After his fall, in 1232, and the rise of his enemy, the Poitevin Peter des Roches, bishop of Winchester, to the place of chief adviser to the crown, the old system of encroachment on the liberties and independence of Scotland was revived.

[1] Hugh de Lusignan, count de la Marche, was to have married her, but preferred the widowed Queen Isabella instead. He continued his custody of the daughter, however, hoping to profit thereby, and it was with difficulty that Henry secured possession of her.

[2] This clause marks the jealousy of a foreign alliance.

[3] Bain, Cal. Docts., I, Nos. 730, 732, 734, 739, 740, 749, 755-6, 758, 761-2, 766; Foedera, I, p. 227; Annal. Dunst., An. 1220; Fordun, Annals, §§ 31, 40.

[4] The marriage of Isabella to Roger le Bigod, son and heir of Hugh, earl of Norfolk, did not take place till the summer of 1225. The third part of all Roger's lands were given her in dower "according to the law and custom of England." The king of Scotland has ward of the lands of Roger till he reaches his majority. (Mt. Paris, Chron. Maj., An. 1221; Bain, Cal. Docts., I, Nos. 803, 806, 808-9, 906, 909, 925, 939, 940, 1002-5. On the reasons for the fall of De Burgh see Early Kings, II, p. 24.)

Meanwhile, however, Alexander was freely exercising his rights as the independent sovereign of Scotland in putting down a revolt in Argyle. In 1234 the death of Alan fitz Roland caused disturbances in Galloway, which were also successfully repressed.[1] The sources furnish fresh proof of an independent Scottish supremacy north of the Solway. Both Alan and his father held English fiefs, but they were first of all devoted to the interests of the king of Scotland, nor did the double relation they sustained[2] in any way

Trouble in Galloway

---

[1] He left three daughters, but no son. The men of Galloway appealed to Alexander to prevent its partition among the heiresses, and rallied around a natural son of Alan. But they were defeated, and the daughters of Alan were confirmed and maintained in their rights by the Scottish king. About the same time Alexander strengthened his interests among the barons who headed the national party in England by giving his youngest sister, Marjory, in marriage to Gilbert the Marshall, earl of Pembroke, the rites being honorably celebrated at Berwick. (Mt. Paris, Chron. Maj., III, pp. 364-5. *Cf.* Early Kings, II, p. 25; Annal. Dunstap., An. 1235.)

[2] The sheriff of Rutland is commanded "to take in the K.'s hand Alan de Galweia's land in Wissendene, which the K. committed to Earl David till Alan did homage to the K." "The justiciar of Ireland is commanded to allow Thomas de Galweia, who has done homage to the K., to hold the lands given him by K. John in Ireland in peace, according to his charters." In answer to a letter of Alan's regarding the lands he held of the English crown Henry writes: "The king has ordered that his lands in Ireland, given by K. John, shall now be restored, and letters to this effect have been sent . . . . to the justiciar of Ireland. The K. farther informs him that he and great part of his council are to meet A[lexander] K. of Scotland, and great part of his council at York at that day (*sic*), to discuss matters relating to their two kingdoms; therefore he directs Alan to come there on the foresaid day, to do his homage and fealty, and grant the charter of his faithful service, and the K. will willingly do regarding Alan's English lands what he ought to do *de jure*." A writ of June 16 orders the sheriff of Rutland to give Alan seizin of his land and its issues from date of first writ, as he has done homage. (Bain, Cal. Docts., I, Nos. 718, 722, 955, 763-4.) These citations again show (1) that homage *preceded* the conferring of fiefs. The process, therefore, had no validity till it was complete. Homage was consequently often expressed vaguely, or with a reservation — "salvo jure suo," and some English historians have claimed such homage by the kings of Scotland as being for their kingdom. It might as properly be claimed that the homage of Alan was for his lands in Galloway, though after the homage his *English* lands are expressly mentioned. They show (2) how intricate the relations between the kingdoms were becoming; how an unscrupulous king in an appeal to the pope, for example, might be tempted to twist the homage of the constable of Scotland for lands in England and Ireland so as to include lands in Scotland. It was only by the exercise of the most scrupulous care, which becomes increasingly manifest, that the perversion of feudal rights was prevented.

affect the independence of the land of their nativity. The attitude of Alexander during these events is in striking contrast with that of William the Lion under Henry II.

The fall of Hubert de Burgh and the death of Richard the Marshall opened the way for a revival of the English claims to supremacy in Scotland. The first act of hostility under the reign of the new favorite, Peter des Roches, was the ratification by the king of an appeal which the archbishop of York

Hostile Policy toward Scotland

.... is about to make .... against A[lexander] K. of Sots having himself crowned, in prejudice, both of the royal dignity and of the liberty of the said archbishop and his church.

The provisions of the treaty of Falaise were adroitly set forth as part of the later agreements between John and William, and drew from Gregory IX a letter favorable to the English cause. The true purpose and character of the transaction have already been exposed; the king's claim had as little basis of right as did that resuscitated by the archbishop of York.[1] Alexander's reply was a demand on the king for the satisfaction of his claims in the north of England. He declares, says Matthew of Paris, that he had charters, witnessed by many of the bishops and chief clergy, and of the earls and barons, certifying that King John had given him "terram Northamhumbriae" with his daughter Joanna "in maritagium;" that it was infamous for a king to annul a pact thus made and witnessed. He added that unless what approved itself as his evident right should be granted peaceably, he would demand it with the sword. Many of the English barons sided with Alexander, declaring his cause just, and reminding Henry of the dangers which threatened him in Wales and France. Both parties finally agreed to remain at peace till an equitable settlement could be reached. In the interim John "the Scot," earl of Chester, Lincoln, and Huntingdon, died. The king of Scotland received seizin of the honor of Huntingdon, and other lands, which John had held of him as

[1] Bain, Cal. Docts., I, Nos. 1154, 1181, 1265–6; *cf.* No. 1277; Early Kings, II, pp. 30–1, 418, 420; Foedera (Record Ed.), I, Pt. I, pp. 214, 215, 233; Pt. II, p. 932.

tenant-in-capite—four manors being excepted, which the earl held directly of the king of England.[1]

Settlement of the Northern Claims

On the 13th of August, 1237, Henry wrote to the archbishop of York that he was coming to treat of peace with Alexander, but that he would not be able to go as far as Durham, on account of the legate, whom he wished to be present at the conference. Nor indeed could Durham "hold such a multitude of people, nor would they find victuals." The archbishop and others were to meet the king of Scots as usual and conduct him to York. Here, on September 25, an agreement was reached between Henry, king of England, and Alexander, king of Scotland, "respecting all claims made by, or competent to, the latter, up to Friday next before Michaelmas A. D. 1237." This agreement, ratified in the most solemn manner by the barons and clergy of England and Scotland, is as follows:

The K. of Scotland quitclaims to the K. of England, his hereditary rights to the counties of Northumberland, Cumberland, and Westmoreland, forever; also 15,000 marks of silver paid by his late father K. William to John K. of England, for certain conventions, not observed by the latter; also frees him of the agreements between the said K. John and K. William, respecting the marriages to be made between the said K. Henry or Richard his brother, and Margaret or Isabella, sisters of the said Alexander; and likewise of the agreements between the said K. Henry and Alexander regarding the marriage to be contracted between the said Henry, and Marjory sister of said Alexander. Henry on the other hand grants to Alexander 200 librates of land within Northumberland and Cumberland, if they can be found outside vills, where castles are placed, or in other competent places adjacent to these counties; to be held by Alexander and his successors kings of Scotland, for the yearly reddendo of a 'soar' [one year old] hawk at Carlisle by the hands of the Constable for the time of the castle, at the feast of the Assumption of the Blessed Mary, for all demands. The kings of Scotland to hold the lands with sok and sak, tholl and theam, infangenethef, utfangenethef, hamsokne, grithbrech, blothwyt, fyghtwyt, ferdwyt, hongwyt', leyrwyt', flemensefrith', murder

[1] Mt. Paris, Chron. Maj., III, pp. 372, 394, 413; Bain, I, Nos. 1325–9, 1333.

and larceny, forstall', within time and without, everywhere. He and his heirs, and their men of said lands, are to be free of all scot, geld, aids of sheriffs, and their servants, hidage, carucage, danegeld, horngeld, hostings, wapentakes, scutages, lestages, stallages, shires, hundreds, wards, warthpeny, averpeny, hundredespenny, borgalpeny, tething peny; and of all works of castles, bridges, park enclosings, and all 'kareio, summagio, navigio, building of palaces, etc. They shall have all 'wayf' animals found on their lands, unless the owner follows and proves his property. All pleas hereafter arising, and wont to be held before the Justices *in banco*, or before the K. himself on his Eyre, shall hereafter be pled in the K. of Scotland's court within said lands, and be determined by his bailiffs, by the return of the K. of England's writ, delivered by his sheriffs to said bailiffs, if such pleas can be held and determined by the law of England. Pleas not determinable before the said bailiffs, shall be held and determined before the K. of England's Justices errant, at their first assize within the county where the lands lie, before any other pleas are held, as shall be just, the Steward of the K. of Scotland being present and sitting as a Justice. The bailiffs or men of the K. of Scotland, shall not go out of said counties where the lands lie for any summons or plea. Should any of the land assigned be within a forest, no forester of the K. of England shall enter to eat, or house himself, or exact anything, except for attachments of pleas of the forest, and by view of the K. of Scotland's bailiff if required. Pleas of the Crown arising in the lands, shall be attached by the bailiffs and coroners of the K. of England, in the presence (if desired) of fhe K. of Scotland's bailiff, and shall be determined by the said Justices errant and the foresaid steward, at the first assize as aforesaid. In other pleas, justice shall be done, after trial, on any man of the said lands, by the bailiffs of the K. of Scotland; the said K. not having power to remit any punishment according to law, nor to restore to the heirs of criminals, land lost by felony, nor to remit amercements for forfeiture. All other amercements and escheats of said lands, and all other issues arising therefrom, shall remain to the K. of Scotland and his heirs; and should he or they be ever impleaded for the lands, the K. of Engand shall warrant and defend them. The K. of Scotland is not to appear, or answer for such suit to anyone, in an English court of law. The Scottish K. makes his homage and fealty—*de praedictis terris*. All writings on the above matters between the late or present Kings of England and Scotland, to be severally restored; but any clauses in them not touching the same, but for the good of either kingdom, are to be renewed; and any charters found regarding the said counties are to be restored to the K. of England.¹

As a result of this convention, Henry directed his agents at Bamburgh and Newcastle-on-Tyne to spend as little as possible on fortifications, "as a firm peace has been entered upon . . . . , so that now the king is not in fear of his castles as before." The justiciar of Ireland is also to allow all the Scottish merchants to come and trade in Ireland freely. A writ was soon issued ordering certain men of England to meet the "*estimatores*" of the king of Scots at Carlisle, "there to swear that they will faithfully value the 200 librates of land to be assigned to A[lexander] K. of Scots." But it was difficult to reach an agreement, Henry naturally wishing to give as little as possible, and Alexander insisting on a complete fulfilment of the treaty. There are numerous entries on the subject. In November, 1240, Henry instructs the "custos" of the bishopric of Durham, "out of the issues of the same," to cause the king of Scotland to have 400l., "in recompence of the arrears of land which the K. is bound to assign, but has not yet assigned to him." On the 16 of February, 1241, the king empowers the bishop of Durham to assign Alexander lands in Cumberland, Westmoreland, and Northumberland, to the amount of "200l. librates of land." On the 20th Henry commands him, "if the K. of Scots is unwilling to receive the 200l. librates of land to be assigned by the bishop, to assign him lands or liberties to the additional amount of 20 librates, unless by chance he is content with the less amount. Gives the Bishop full powers." In April, 1242, the

¹ The papal legate proposed to enter Scotland after the conclusion of the treaty. Alexander replied that neither in his time nor in those of this antecessors had any legate (for England) had such entrance, nor would he tolerate it now. Odo, therefore, returned to the south with Henry. In this connection Innocent IV decreed that ecclesiastical causes arising within the kingdom of Scotland, "shall not be tried by the Legates out of its bounds. But should the Roman See for any lawful reason ordain that such should be tried out of Scotland, they are not to be tried in the city or diocese of York, but only in Carlisle or Durham, as being nearer Scotland." (Mt. Paris, Chron. Maj., III, p. 414; Bain, Cal. Docts., I, Nos. 1349, 1358, 1675; Foedera, I, p. 376.)

claims which the Scottish kings had steadily maintained as their right and inheritance were conceded and settled by a grant to Alexander of "the manors of Langwadeby, Saleghild, Scottheby, Scoureby, Carlanton, and sixty librates of land to be extended and assigned to him in the K.'s manor of Penrith, with all their liberties and free customs." A writ was also issued for payment to Alexander "of 300l. for his arrears of 200 librates of land which the king ought to have assigned to him."[1]

Soon after the conference at York, Alexander's, wife Joanna, died, leaving him without heirs. Two years later he married Marry de Coucy, daughter of a great French baron, and in 1241 Alexander III was born—the last direct male heir to the throne of Scotland by the conjoined lines of MacAlpin and Cerdic.[2]

In 1242 Henry was drawn into war with Louis IX of France, through the influence of his Poitevin advisers. Before undertaking it he tightened the bonds uniting himself and the king of Scots, by making a complete settlement of the claims adjusted at York, and by betrothing his daughter Margaret to the infant heir of Alexander. The custody of the English marches was also entrusted to the king of the Scots. During Henry's absence, an event occurred which came near interrupting the peaceful relations between the kingdoms of England and Scotland. Walter Bisset, a powerful baron of Norman descent, was banished from Scotland for an atrocious murder. Repairing to Henry's court, he declared he was the victim of a faction over which Alexander had no control, and artfully insinuated that the latter had no right to deprive him of his lands in Scotland without Henry's consent. He alleged also that the king of Scotland, in violation of his fealty, had received

Walter Bisset

---

[1] Bain, Cal. Docts., I, Nos. 1362-4, 1440, 1442, 1506, 1512, 1570-3, 1575-7, 1612.

[2] Mt. Paris, Chron. Maj., III, pp. 479, 530; Fordun, An., §44; Bain, I, Nos. 1405-7; Early Kings, II, p. 33, note. Henry writes Alexander that "although the business between him and the sister of the Queen of the K. (*sic*) [of England ?] cannot attain the effect wished, yet he desires that so great a league may unite and conjoin them, that in all their doings they may be mutually stronger." (Bain, I, No. 1444.) Henry married Alienora, daughter of Raymond Berenger IV, count of Provence, in January, 1236. (*Cf.* Mt. Paris, Chron. Maj.)

in his land Geoffrey de Marisco, a fugitive from justice. Alexander had given no ground for complaint, but his marriage with Mary de Coucy, a French woman, and therefore supposedly hostile to English interests, had occasioned a certain coolness of feeling between the kings, which now culminated. Henry had returned from Poitou in disgrace, and his weak nature was peculiarly open to Bisset's insinuations. He secretly secured aid from his wife's uncle, the count of Flanders. He also *commanded* the Irish king, Dovenald, to join the justiciar of Ireland—"who is shortly to set out for Scotland with the K.'s Irish lieges"—*in person*, with such force as he could bring. Similar writs were sent to twenty of the Irish chieftains. His attitude to Ireland and Wales shows they occupied a position radically different from that of Scotland—including both Lothian and Galloway—the latter being clearly independent.

In the summer of 1244 Henry concentrated his entire military force on Newcastle-on-Tyne. Alexander's father-in-law, Engelram, had recently died, and the troops sent by his son were intercepted by the English. But in his subjects the king of Scotland found a bulwark of strength. A thousand knights and about 100,000 infantry gathered about the king, prepared to die for their country's *just cause*.[1] Alexander had anticipated Henry's attack by establishing himself in a fortified camp at Ponteland, a little north of Newcastle, where he could observe the movements of his antagonist. But the barons of England who were so closely bound to both kingdoms, were little inclined to war. They had a warm regard for the king of Scotland, and his resolute bearing warned them of a dangerous and doubtful conflict. They were indignant at sight of the contemptible contingent from Flanders. The national spirit resented John's policy of reliance on foreigners. An attitude of peace was the normal condition of feeling toward Scotland at this time. Negotiations were, therefore, easily set on foot. Paris describes Alexander as "vir bonus, justus, pius, dapsilis, ab omnibus tam

---

[1] This from an English chronicler, Mt. Paris. He is the best representative of the growing national spirit.

Anglis quam suis diligabatur, *et merito*." It is easy to infer on which side justice lay. Henry's charges against Alexander were that some of his nobles had built two castles in Galloway and Lothian, to the prejudice of the English crown and the security of English lieges on the borders; that by sheltering Geoffrey de Marisco and other fugitives, he had shown an intention of withdrawing his homage and allying with France. The charters which were mutually exchanged indicate that Henry received no satisfaction except on the subject of the foreign alliance, which was undoubtedly the real point at issue.[1] Alexander bound himself and his heirs to keep the peace to his "liege lord," Henry III and his heirs; he would enter into no treaty of war against the dominions of the English king, unless in requital of injuries. The conventions lately entered into at York, as well as those regarding the intended marriage between Alexander's son and Henry's daughter, were confirmed. As one of the disputed castles, the Hermitage, in Liddesdale, remained standing, and no mention is made regarding the delivery of fugitives, these points were apparently quietly dropped by Henry's representatives as beyond his jurisdiction. Alexander's rights having in turn been guaranteed against aggression, the two armies retired from the frontier, the fortified camp at Ponteland was given up, and the kingdoms were again at peace.[2]

Features of Alexander's Reign

During Alexander's reign the records of the English court portray afresh the anomalous condition of the king of Scots and those of his nobles who held fiefs south of the Tweed and Solway—at once dependent and independent. Where a conflict of service arose, the Scottish vassals seem invariably to have been excused from service for their English fiefs, that they might first

---

[1] A writ of April 20, 1244, commands the sheriffs of the northern counties "to make close search if any one from beyond seas, knight, merchant or other stranger, passes to Scotland, or any one from Scotland to parts beyond seas; and to arrest any such person bearing arms, or letters of a suspicious nature, and send him to the K." (Bain, I, No. 1631.)

[2] Mt. Paris, Chron. Maj., IV, pp. 200, 359, 361, 379; Bain, I, Nos. 1637, 1703, 1836, 1865, 1640–6, 1648, 1654–5, 1650; Early Kings, II, pp. 38, 40, 42; Foedera, I, p. 429; II, p. 216.

serve their king. If war arose between the kingdoms their fiefs, forfeited by supporting their primary lord, the king of Scotland, were usually restored on the return of peace. The invasion of the fealty of subjects on either side is carefully guarded against. Gifts of money are not to be wrongfully construed. The king of England

.... declares that the aid of 2000 marks which A[lexander] K. of Scotland has made at his instance against his transfretation this year, proceeds entirely from that K.'s liberality; and that this present, thus freely made, is not to be hereafter drawn maliciously by any into a precedent.[1]

There is a noticeable tendency on the part of border barons to have their charters for possessions near the line confirmed by both kings, especially in case of a transfer of property.[2]

The K. (Henry) ratifies the lease (ballium) and grant made by Robert de Muschans to Boidin de Argu of his manor of Chevelingeham [Chillingham in Northumberland], to be held till the said Robert shall cause Boydyn to have seizin of a carucate and a half of land, three oxgangs and 6 acres of meadow, and a mill in Halsinton, confirmed by Robert to Boydyn by charter, in the said manor in Scotland.

An interesting glimpse of the method of holding parliaments at this early period is revealed in the order of the king of England to let the nuns of Newcastle-on-Tyne have thirty quarters of wheat "for the damages sustained by them in their crops trodden down (conculcatis) by the Parliament lately held outside of said town." Seventeen parties in Northumberland are similarly remunerated for losses to their crops on account of the parliament between the kings of England and Scotland.

One of the most important features of this reign is the development of "March law"—and an attempt to fix the line between the two kingdoms. In 1222, at a meeting of duly

---

[1] The apparent ease with which Alexander obtained money, and the poverty of Henry throughout his reign, are in striking contrast.

[2] Bain, Cal. Docts., I, Nos. 693, 818, 822, 970, 1041, 1241, 1295, 895, 909, 914, 1066, 1086, 1096, 1105, 1101, 1128, 1113, 832, 1676, 1699, 1749, 1765, 1776.

appointed knights of Northumberland and Scotland, an attempt was made to get "a true perambulation between the kingdoms, viz., between Karham and Hawedene." The six English knights, as jurors, "with one assent proceeded by the right and ancient marches between the kingdoms," declaring on oath that they were "from Tweed, by the rivulet of Revedenburne, ascending toward the south as far as 'Tres Karras,' and from thence in a straight line ascending as far as Hoperichelawe, and from thence in a straight line to Witelawe." The Scotch knights totally dissented from this view and threatened to prevent such perambulation by force. Twenty-three years later the matter again came up, the purpose being to make settlement of "the lands in dispute between the Canons of Karham in England, and Bernard de Haudene in Scotland."[1] The line formerly declared to be the true one was agreed on in the presence of several English justices, the justiciar of Lothian, the sheriff of Roxburgh, and others representing both sides in the case. In 1248 a restatement of the March law was made. The king of England, having heard from the envoys of the king of Scotland "that the laws and customs of the Marches of the Kingdoms in the time of their predecessors, Kings of England and Scotland, hitherto used, were now less well observed," and that "injury had been done to Nicholas de Sules against said laws," ordered the sheriff of Northumberland "to cause the same to be inviolably kept, and to give redress to said Nicholas if found due." Certain knights of England and Scotland, having assembled at the March on Tweed under the precepts of their respective kings

. . . . for the purpose of correcting offences against said march laws and customs, did duly correct, according to the ancient and approved custom of the March, such matters as required redress. And it was proposed on the part of the K. of Scotland that Nicholas de Soules had been injured by being impleaded before the K. of England for transgressions by his men of Scotland dwelling in Scotland, perpetrated in England. The said knights, having carefully inquired

[1] Bain, No. 832.

into the matter by the elder and more discreet persons on both sides of the March, according to ancient march law and custom, say that the said Nicholas has been injured by being so impleaded elsewhere than at the march, although he holds land in England; for no one of either kingdom, although holding lands in both, is liable by March law, to be impleaded anywhere but at the march, for any deed by his men dwelling in England, done in Scotland; or for any deed by his men dwelling in Scotland, done in England.

This statement makes it very clear that the same rules applied with equal force to the subjects of both kingdoms; that *the holding of lands in England* was the sole ground for submitting to the jurisdiction of English courts; and that *even under such circumstances* the case in question *must be tried at the March*. It well illustrates the proposition already set forth that the kingdom of Scotland was independent, and that any appearances to the contrary were occasioned by the peculiar relations which the king of the north, and a considerable number of his subjects, sustained to the lord of their English fiefs.

CHAPTER VIII.

THE REIGN OF ALEXANDER III.

Five days after the death of Alexander II his son was crowned at Scone. There were some who opposed, on the ground that the day was unlucky, and that the boy of eight years had not yet been knighted — an honor, the conferring of which Alan Durward, the justiciar of Scotland, coveted for himself. But Walter Comyn, earl of Menteith, a man of foresight and power, and a loyal friend of the deceased king, urged that delay was fatal, that knighthood was not a prerequisite to kingship, and that the interests of Scotland demanded an immediate coronation. His arguments prevailed, and the consecration of the king ensued upon the ancient Stone of Destiny. The coronation ceremonies revealed the leaders of the two parties, whose strife and dissension made it possible for the king of England to intervene in Scotland as "Principal Adviser" to the child husband of his daughter. Walter Comyn, whose family was said to include at that time "two earls and upwards of thirty knights," headed the national or Scottish party. The southern barons, whose leaning toward England is not to be wondered at, were led by Alan Durward, the justiciar, Bruce, lord of Annandale, the steward, and others. Menteith's promptness foiled Henry's purpose to prevent the crowning of Alexander without his consent, while the pope administered a merited rebuke for his efforts to have the coronation set aside, and for seeking tithes of the ecclesiastical revenues of Scotland, in addition to those of England and Ireland, for a crusade.[1]

Alexander III, 1249-1285

---

[1] Fordun, §§ 47-8; Early Kings, II, pp. 53 ff.; Bain, I, Nos. 1798, 1806, 2014. Innocent IV, to the king of England: "In reply to his request, that the K. of Scotland, since he is his liegeman and does homage to him, may not be anointed or

As the summer of 1251 began to wane, preparations were made for the marriage of Alexander and Margaret, in accordance with the agreements previously made. Everything was on the most sumptuous scale. Writs were issued for 5,000 hens, 1,500 partridges, with cranes, swans, peacocks, pheasants, hares, rabbits, swine, and salmon, in proportion. Five hundred bucks and does, well salted, were to be at York against the marriage at Christmas, and 132 casks of wine. Rich presents of jewels, gold, and silver, are daily recorded as in making; beautiful robes in abundance, among others one for the king, of the best violet samnite, "with three small leopards on the front, and three others behind." A fair sword, and silver-gilt spurs, "with silken ligaments, becomingly and ornately made," were to be ready for the knighting of the heir to the throne of Scotland. When this ceremony and the marriage rites had been performed, Alexander rendered homage to Henry in the usual way, and received investment of his fiefs in England. Matthew Paris says the homage was "ratione tenementi, quod tenet de domino rege Anglorum, de regno scilicet Angliae, Laudiano videlicet et terris reliquis." When Henry urged homage for the kingdom of Scotland as well, Alexander replied that he had come thither at the request of the king on a peaceful and honorable mission, viz., that they might be allied by marriage, and not to treat of arduous matters of state — in which he would require the advice of his council. Henry, perhaps ashamed of his attempt to take advantage of a child, ceased to urge the matter. The Earl Marshall was also forbidden to press his claims to the palfrey of the king of Scotland.[1]

Alexander Marries Henry's Daughter

This narrative is specially significant because it comes from a monk of St. Albans, whose chroniclers strenuously uphold the

crowned, without his consent, the K. is not to wonder if the Apostolic See, which is unaccustomed to such demands, does not grant it, as greatly lessening the [Scottish] K.'s dignity. The K. also is not to be disturbed at the Pope refusing to grant him the tithe of ecclesiastical benefices in Scotland; for it is altogether unheard of, that this should be given to anyone in the kingdom of another."

[1] Mt. Paris, Chron. Maj., V, p. 266; Bain I, No. 1815 ff.

feudal supremacy of England in Scotland. It shows how one attempt against the independence of the kingdom was frustrated.

Paris' statement that Lothian was among the fiefs for which homage was rendered cannot be accepted. It seems to be an echo from Wendover's fictitious account of the cession of this district to Kenneth II by Edgar, in 975. It was *claimed* as an English fief by some of the chroniclers, just as the Scots, a few years after the capture of William the Lion, *claimed* that his homage was for Lothian and not for the kingdom of Scotland. Both claims were equally false. Alexander III did *not* do homage for the *kingdom of Scotland*, by Paris' own testimony. This is the really important point. And if Lothian had been an English earldom, as Palgrave and Freeman state, on exactly the same footing as Tynedale, and homage had been done for it, as Paris intimates, it must have been included, like Tynedale, in the compotus of the lands of which Alexander received seizin, after the homage at York. But it is not mentioned. Moreover, if Malcolm IV surrendered Lothian with the northern counties to Henry II, as the St. Albans chroniclers state, how does it now appear as one of the English fiefs held by the Scottish king? When was it restored to him? In lieu of his surrender, Malcolm received the honor of Huntingdon. And after the Barons' war (1217) Alexander II was seized only of this honor and the lands connected with it in nine counties. But these were all south of the Humber and could not have included Lothian. A little later Alexander II received the grant in Cumberland in commutation of all his claims on the northern counties. Lothian is not included in the grant, nor among the counties claimed, for which the grant was made. And yet, according to Paris, it *is* among the English lands which Alexander II held, for which Alexander III did homage and was given seizin. The utter silence of the best sources regarding Lothian, and their explicit testimony regarding all the English lands held by the king of Scotland, expose the error of Paris and the falsity of the entire conception of Lothian as an English earldom — in which, however, English justices have no place, from which the barons are never summoned to do the service they render for their specified lands in Northumberland and elsewhere, and for which the sheriffs make no account at the Exchequer, as they always do for Tynedale and other English lands held by Scottish kings or nobles. It was an integral part of the kingdom of Scotland.[1]

The question of homage having been settled for the time, the king promised to pay to Alexander, within four years, 5,000 marks of silver, as the "maritagium" of his daughter Margaret; he would thus "be freed from said amount, as contained in the writings between the K. and Alexander's father."[2] The bailiffs of the king of Scotland there present, at his own instance, then spontaneously restored their bailiaries to him. Fearing, however, that such an act done outside the kingdom of Scotland might be wrongly construed, they required and received from the king of England letters under his seal, that "no prejudice to the K. and kingdom of Scotland" should hereafter arise because of their act.

For some years after Alexander's return to the north, Henry's troubles in Gascony, and with his refractory nobles in England, did not permit of interference in the kingdom of Scotland. He also wished to establish his son Edmund as king of Sicily, with papal sanction. Alexander IV, seeking an ally in the king of England against the Emperor Frederic, had granted to Henry what Innocent had stigmatized as "an unprecedented request"—a twentieth of the revenues of the Church of Scotland. Henry declared, however, by writ, "that no prejudice shall hereafter arise to A[lexander], K. of Scotland, or his heirs by reason of the grant by the pope to the English K. of the twentieth of ecclesiastical benefices in Scotland in aid of the Holy Land, for three years."

Returns to Scotland

---

[1] Bain, Cal. Docts., I, Nos. 1790, 1799, 1855, 1857.

[2] Henry was always embarrassed financially. He complains of being at "intolerable expense." A payment of 500 marks "drained" the Exchequer. In 1270 he still owed 2,000 marks. (Bain, I, Nos. 1848, 1851, 2295, 2589. *Cf.* also Fordun, An., §50; Mt. Paris, Chron. Maj., An. 1252.)

The attitude of the pope is well shown in letters to Rostannus, his chaplain and envoy in England:

Desires him to enjoin the prelates and other dignified clergy of Scotland to afford liberal aid to the Pope to defray his debts incurred in the affairs of Sicily; in which case his Holiness will remit the papal twentieth granted to the K. of England in aid of the Holy Land. If they do not, he is to collect the twentieth without delay. If he has to take proceedings, he is to keep silence as to any privileges or indulgences to the Scottish Church, or the question of its independence.

And under the same date (1250),

Though the Pope has remitted to the prelates the twentieth of ecclesiastical benefices in Scotland, granted to the K. of England, yet the redemptions of vows of crusaders, uncertain bequests, and offerings arising from whatever cause, in aid of the Holy Land, should be collected for the said K.'s use. He accordingly commands his envoy to collect the same, under the above reservations as to secrecy.[1]

Since the meeting at York, the Scottish national party, headed by Walter Comyn, earl of Menteith, had been in control in Scotland. Alan Durward represented the faction of nobles who, though holding fiefs in both kingdoms, and primarily subjects of the king of Scotland, were yet of southern blood, and favored Henry's interests. Yet both parties, in their fiercest strife, resented any encroachment on their rights, and Henry's interference in Scotland was tolerated only on his repeated assurances, in writing, that he meditated no harm against the liberties of the kingdom, seeking only the interests of his son-in-law and daughter, till they should attain their majority.

Parties in Scotland

A variety of events, ending in a skilfully laid plot, gave the English party possession of the young king and queen of Scotland, and the national party was defied to attack the castle of Roxburgh while it contained their sovereign lord. Henry summoned his barons and advanced towards the north. As he approached the borders, he wrote:

[1] Bain, Cal. Docts., I, Nos. 1956, 1984-5, 2040, 2065-6; Mt. Paris, Chron. Maj., An. 1255.

The K. understanding that some fear he proposes to weaken the state of Scotland or its liberties, whereas he is under many bonds to maintain the K. of Scotland's honor, and the liberties of his kingdom unhurt, declares that nothing was done on the occasion of the marriage of Alexander and his daughter Margaret at York, concerning the state of his councillors and their bailliaries, calculated to injure his kingdom or its liberties. As he is about to approach the Scottish borders to see the said K. and his daughter, "according to the great desire of his heart," he will neither do, nor permit others to do, anything prejudicial to said K. or his kingdom, but rather, as bound by the link of paternal affection, give all his power and influence, if need be, to preserve the same.

Safe-conducts were issued for the king and queen of Scotland to meet their parents at Werk castle, on the border. But before their departure was permitted, the distinguished delegation of English nobles, who had come as their escort, was compelled to

.... guarantee that neither the K. or Queen, or any of their followers, shall tarry in England, save with consent of all the magnates of Scotland, and that they will permit nothing to be done in prejudice of the Scottish king or his kingdom or its liberties.

A similar document from the king of England confirmed the pledge of the nobles. At the instance of his father-in-law and "the council of his own magnates," as now constituted, the king of Scotland removed the former regents from his council, and made entirely new appointments. In the event of a foreign invasion they were to be restored to favor. The provisions agreed upon at this meeting were embodied in letters, which were to remain in force till the king of Scotland attained his majority, the king of England promising that on the expiration of the term specified "no prejudice should arise to him or his kingdom thereby." Thus the English party in Scotland reached the height of its power. But it by no means voiced the national sentiment, represented by Menteith and the bishops of St. Andrews and Glasgow, who "incurred the vehement displeasure of Henry for openly refusing to affix their seals to a document which they stigmatized as infamous." They were to triumph in the end.[1]

The new regents initiated their reign by calling their predecessors to account. As the defeated party absolutely refused to acknowledge the authority of their rivals, the kingdom of Scotland was filled with strife; Gamelin, bishop-elect of St. Andrews, and chancellor under the first regents, especially suffered. Though at length consecrated to his see, he gained little advantage from it, being banished from the realm because he refused to yield to the extortionate demands of the party in power. The pope warmly espoused his cause, urging Henry to use his influence to have these wrongs redressed. "He has heard with grief that some of the K. of Scotland's 'so-called' councillors, who might rather be called 'assentators,' have turned his tender mind by crafty and evil advice, and that G[amelin], bishop of St. Andrews, is spoiled of his goods, and driven in exile from his church, to the no light injury and contempt of the Holy Name, and his apostle." The appeal apparently brought no immediate results, though it was in time to have an important bearing on affairs in Scotland.[2]

Meanwhile preparations were made for the entertainment of the king and queen of Scotland, on a visit to their parents in England. It was to be a purely social meeting. A safe-conduct provided that neither the king nor his friends should " be spoken to on any matters touching himself or his kingdom against his will." The sheriff of York was to pay to Alexander, from the issues of his county, " 100l., for the 100s. which he is wont to draw daily from the K. for his expenses, so often as he comes to England at the K.'s command." On Alexander's return to Scotland, an unexpected opportunity presented itself to the national party. The pope, mindful of the interests of his protégé Gamelin, directed the bishop of Dunblane and the abbots of Melrose and Jedburgh to excommunicate the regents, if they

[1] Bain, Cal. Docts., I, Nos. 1966, 1986, 1988, 1990, 1992, 1995, 2002, 2004, 2012, 2013; Mt. Paris, Chron. Maj., V, pp. 501, 504, 507, 556. *Cf.* Early Kings, II, pp. 63, 67, 73.
[2] Bain, I, No. 2037.

persisted in keeping him out of his see of St. Andrews. The national party could now justify themselves in rescuing their sovereign from the hands of excommunicated traitors, which they succeeded in doing on the night of October 28, 1257. Efforts for a compromise had already been set on foot; the national party used their victory wisely, and after some bluster on Henry's part, the strife of parties was appeased. A council made up of four from either side, with the queen mother of Scotland and her husband, was agreed on. It included among others Gamelin, the Comyn earls of Menteith and Buchan, and Alan Durward. It was really a victory for the Comyn party, for they retained all the great offices of state in their hands, including the justiciarship of Lothian. Henry gave his approval to the new arrangements, promising his counsel and aid, if required, so long as affairs should be conducted "according to God and justice, the honour and advantage of the K. and Queen of Scotland, and the old laws and customs of that realm."[1]

In the fall of 1260 a number of causes called the king of Scotland to the south. Westminster says he wished to look after his interests in the county of Huntingdon, to demand payment of the balance of his wife's marriage dower, and to claim certain lands between the Tyne and Wentsbeck.[2] The queen also wished to be with her mother. Safe-conducts were granted in August by Henry and Prince Edward, providing that the king and his councillors should not be addressed on matters of state without his consent. No disturbance was to be made by the king of England in the state of the king of Scotland or his councillors and other attendants while in England. Should he or his queen or any of their retinue fall sick, their safe conduct was to remain in force

Birth of Margaret

---

[1] Bain, Cal. Docts., I, Introd., p. xlii, Nos. 2053–6, 2062–3, 2083–4, 2090, 2103–4, 2114, 2121, 2125, 2128, 2131; Mt. Paris, Chron. Maj., V, p. 576; *cf.* Early Kings, II, pp. 71–3; also Bain, I, Nos. 2133, 2139–40, 2155–7. The earl of Menteith was killed by a fall from a horse, in November, 1258. (*Cf.* Early Kings, II, p. 80, and Mt. Paris, Chron. Maj., V, pp. 724, 739.)

[2] On the border of Cumberland, Westmoreland, and Northumberland. (Early Kings, II, p. 82, note; Mt. West., II, p. 388.)

one month after convalescence. Should the queen become pregnant in England, neither she nor her child, if born there, should be detained. Should either die, the other was to be freely restored to Scotland. Should the king, the child's father, die meanwhile, "or other unforeseen event occur to him," the leading men in the Scottish national party were to receive the child and take it to Scotland. Alexander returned to the north after a time, granting the request of the king and queen of England, that their daughter might remain with them for a season. But so jealously did the Scots guard against any mischance that they required fresh assurances from Henry, confirmed by his brother Richard, and the magnates of his realm, of his honorable intentions. In February, Margaret gave birth to a daughter, who received her own name, and eventually became the wife of Eric, king of Norway.[1]

Alexander Reaches His Majority

The attainment of his majority released Alexander from the control of his regents, and left him free to carry out his father's policy of annexing the western islands to his own dominions. This he apparently attempted to accomplish by peaceful negotiations with the king of Norway, but the continued attacks of the western lords of Scotland on the lords of the isles occasioned an expedition under the leadership of the aged King Haco, and a brief period of hostility between the subjects, if not between the kings, of the two realms. Under Haco's son, Magnus, peaceful negotiations were renewed, and speedily brought to a successful issue — the ancient kingdom of the isles being transferred to the king of Scotland for 4,000 marks sterling, and an annual subsidy of 100 marks.[2]

On the south also there was peace. A son had been born to the king of Scotland, who received his father's name, and there was rejoicing in the land. When peace was made between Henry and his barons, he granted as hostages his son Edward

[1] Bain, Cal. Docts., I, Nos. 2198, 2205-8, 2229, 2248.
[2] Bain, Cal. Docts., I, Nos. 2320, 2336, 2351, 2355; Early Kings, II, pp. 83 ff.; Fordun An., § 56.

and the son of Richard of Cornwall, titular head of the Holy Roman empire. Writing to Alexander in regard to procuring their release, he admirably sets forth the true relations existing between Scotland and England at this time. He

.... knows by his [Alexander's] frequent letters that he is concerned for the tranquillity of this kingdom [England] and the liberation of Edward, and feels the ties of blood and affinity between them, and their need of mutual help, seeing the near contiguity of their lands. Ernestly begs him to send some of his lieges duly empowered in the above matters, lest the Prince's deliverance be delayed. Hopes his magnates, and others of his land will be induced to aid those of England, if another disturbance arises, and that he will urge those who are not yet bound, to do so.

He also sends messengers to urge the same *viva voce*, and commands his daughter, the queen, to use her influence with the king and his magnates to the same end. It was not thus Edward I addressed the vassal king of Scotland, John Balliol. These letters depict an independent kingdom, bound to another by ties of blood relationship and a complex feudal tenure. The king himself holds lands in England. The queen receives the commands of her father. Some of the magnates of the north owe service for fiefs south of the border. They are urged to give their aid in person in case of future disturbance, and the assistance of others who are under no obligation for English fiefs is earnestly solicited. But there is no intimation of a dependent kingdom subject to the commands of an English overlord. The true nature of the service rendered by Scottish barons appears in a grant by Henry to John Comyn, "on account of the late disturbance in the kingdom," of lands "in the counties beyond the Trent" to the extent of 300 librates, which "he will make up to him before all others." Pleasant relations continued during the remaining years of Henry's reign, there being frequent interchange of social intercourse between the royal families. At the same time, Alexander quietly but firmly maintained his rights against all encroachments.[1]

[1] Bain, Cal. Docts., I, Nos. 2377–9, 2462–3, 2482–3, 2486, 2519, 2542. On the

The news of Henry's death reached his son Edward, who had gone on a crusade, at Capua, early in 1273. He tarried in Italy to see the pope and get permission to levy a tenth on the incomes of the English clergy for three years; at Paris, to do homage to his overlord, Philip III; and in Gascony for upwards of a year. In 1274 he arrived in England and was crowned, his sister Margaret and her husband, the king of Scotland, being present to witness the ceremony. 175l. were granted to Alexander out of the first issues of the bishopric of Durham, in lieu of the corrody of 100s. daily in "coming to Westminster at the K.'s mandate and thence to his own country." Edward assured him that this visit should not form a precedent injurious to himself or his kingdom. The death of the beautiful and loved Margaret shortly after seems to have wrought no change in the relations between her husband and brother. Alexander continued to maintain both his public and private rights. He asks that the bailiffs of Bristol shall release certain Scottish sailors and their goods, arrested on suspicion of piracy. The request is granted. He promises to do justice regarding the plunder of some merchants by sea-robbers, who were said to have a refuge in Scotland, "according to the laws and customs of his own realm." As to collecting an aid for Edward within the liberty of Tynedale, he "cannot reply thereto plainly without first consulting his magnates." In 1276 considerable correspondence occurs regarding Scottish encroachments at Berwick-on-Tweed, which at this time was a prominent center of commerce — "a second Alexandria." The bishop of Durham, in a letter to the king, declares that

Accession of Edward I

.... though the straight course of the Twede is the March *between the kingdoms,* .... yet the justiciars and bailiffs of the K. of Scotland, with a multitude of the men of Berwyk, have crossed the said river at Twedemuthe, and hold courts and outlawries on land once covered by the sea and waves, as if the same belonged to Scotland.

attempt of Ottabone, the papal legate, to levy tithes on beneficiaries in Scotland for the use of Henry in the crusades, *cf.* Early Kings, II, pp. 106 ff., and Bain, I, Nos. 2558-9, 2563-4, 2646; *cf.* also note at end of this chapter.

Some of the burgesses had also arrested in the bishop's liberty, and imprisoned in Berwick, one of the bishop's men. The king instructs the sheriff of Northumberland, if amends are not made, to arrest Scots passing through or staying in his bailliary, till satisfaction is made. Alexander writes to Edward, promising to "treat regarding the controversies on the March according to the laws, usages, and customs hitherto in use." The king of England then commands the bishop " that if the K. of Scotland and his men keep on their own side of the river, he is to endeavor to maintain the peace." Edward carefully scrutinized the rights and privileges conferred on the Scottish king, and confirmed them rather grudgingly. He also pushed his rights as feudal lord of Scottish nobles holding English fiefs to their utmost limit. For example, Alexander Comyn, earl of Buchan, was summoned for service in the Welsh wars. An engagement in the service of the king of Scotland took precedence, as usual, but his son Roger was sent in his stead.[1]

It is pleasant to catch, in passing, a glimpse of the home life of the royal families. Mingled with affairs of state are references to the health of the queen and "the children." Alexander's second son, David, died at the age of ten. But Alexander, the first-born, and his sister, the princess Margaret, write to their big uncle — their "most hearty" and "very dear uncle" — in terms of the warmest affection. Nor can it be doubted that underneath all the statecraft and diplomacy of that era there was a current of blood-relationship and love which had an influence in the destinies of these neighboring kingdoms.[2]

For some unexplained reason, the question of homage did

---

[1] Bain, Cal. Docts., II, Nos. 17, 19, 33, 37, 44, 55, 59, 62-3, 82, 90, 104, 111. *Cf.* Nos. 144, 291; Introd., II, p. xi; Foedera, II, pp. 216, 845. That the earl's service was for lands in England is evident from his own letters and those of Alexander to Edward — "auxilium quod vobis debet ratione terrarum quas de vobis tenet infra regnum vestrum." The earl's wife was a daughter of Roger de Quency, through whom she inherited large possessions in England. Bain, II, No. 241, shows that if Alexander sent money to Edward, it was as a gift, and not as an aid from Tynedale. (National MSS. Scot., No. LXIX; Foedera, II, p. 205.)

[2] Bain, II, Nos. 96, 121, 156-7, 164, 185, 204-5.

not come actively to the front for several years after Edward's coronation. The delay was apparently owing to lack of agreement as to the form of homage and the lands for which it was rendered. In 1275 Alexander petitioned the king of England for the rights of his predecessors in Huntingdon and Nottingham, and concerning other rights. In 1277 the king of England "is not to be anxous or moved" over a certain misunderstanding, nor to give credence to any "sinister" reports, as he [Alexander] is "ever ready, and has been, to preserve the K.'s liberties and rights unsullied as his own, and as the K. has promised to do in regard to the latter." Further correspondence ensued, and letters of safe-conduct were granted by the king and his magnates, in March. These were not satisfactory in the north, and the envoys to the court of Edward — having shown them to the king of Scotland and his council — fittingly replied in their behalf to Edward. They state that the king of Scotland

Question of Homage

.... earnestly desires to come to him and do his pleasure in reason. But it would greatly satisfy the people of his realm if he had the usual safe conduct of the English magnates, or at least the K.'s letter, that the coming of the Scottish K. to England should not hereafter injure him or his heirs.

They, therefore, beg that he will grant such letters,

.... in the form of the English Chancery, which they return under the bishop's seal, by the bearer, to be sent back to them by him; granting therein, if it please him, that the K. of Scotland shall go wherever he pleases in England, and that his escort may be the Archbishops of Canterbury and York and the Earls of Gloucester, Warenne, and Lincoln, whom he desires to have.

Accordingly, on the 5th of June, 1278, the king issued letters patent declaring that the safe-conduct granted to the king of Scotland to come to England "should not tend to the future prejudice of that K. or his heirs." On the 12th the safe-conduct was issued. It declared that if any of the king of Scotland's retinue "trespass or incur forfeiture, it is not to be imputed to their K. if he disavow it, nor is the safe conduct to be thereby injured." Another document of the same date makes provision for Alexander's escort in the respective districts through which he is to pass. On the 14th the form of safe-conduct was sent to Warrenne, earl of Surrey, to be executed, sealed, and delivered to the king of Scotland's clerk. From this point there is some confusion as to the exact order of events. Edward had already written to the bishop of Bath and Wells that, as Alexander had indicated his readiness to do homage "absque conditione aliqua," it would be received at London, in "the Quindene of St Michael" (a fortnight after Michaelmas day). Alexander seems to have come to England, being present with Edward in a parliament at Gloucester near the close of June, just before that king crossed over to France. The confusion among the English writers themselves is shown by Triveti, who says that, according to some, homage had been already performed after the coronation in 1274, while others held that the ceremony occurred at the close of the parliament of Gloucester. Both were wrong. If Alexander was with the king in June, he returned to Scotland, for on September 3 he wrote to Edward from Traquair (Trevequayr). On the 15th Edward commands that the price of provisions shall not be unduly raised during the visit of the king of Scotland to England. This, however, is not to be a precedent. On the 29th, according to a memorandum in the Foedera, taken from the Close Rolls (6 Edw. I, m. 5, dorso), homage and fealty were rendered by Alexander to Edward at Westminster in these words: " Ego, Alexander, Rex Scotiae, devenio ligeus homo Domini Edwardi Regis Angliae contra omnes gentes." Edward received this homage "*salvo jure et clamio ejusdem Regis Angliae*, et haeredem suorum, *de homagio praedicti Regis Scotiae*, et haeredem suorum, *de Regno Scotiae, cum inde loqui voluerint.*" The king of Scotland then requested, and the king of England granted, that the oath of fealty should be taken by Robert Bruce, earl of Carrick, in the king's stead. This was done, and confirmed by Alexander in these words: " Ego Alexander, Rex Scotiae, portabo bonam fidem Domino Edwardo Regi Angliae, et haeredibus suis Regibus Angliae, de vita et membris, et terreno honore, et fideliter faciam servitia, *debita de terris et tenementis, quae teneo de Rege Angliae supradicto.*" The phraseology of Alexander's oath, which left the definition of the lands which he held of Edward to his own interpretation, together with Edward's *salvo*, show conclusively that homage or fealty was *not* rendered for the kingdom of Scotland. Other records show that it was distinctly repudiated. That the account given in the memorandum is not by a contemporary writer seems clear. Its unreliable nature is apparent from its statement that this homage was performed in a parliament at Westminster, on Michaelmas day — homage which, according to Edward's own undoubted testimony, was tendered and postponed till nearly three weeks later. The account seems to be a confused version by a late writer, based not on the facts, but on the letter of Edward to the bishop of Bath and Wells. Edward's plans, as outlined in that letter, apparently miscarried. For, in a letter of October 17, given under his own hand — "teste me ipso apud Coberle" — he declared "that Alexander, K. of Scotland, came before him at Teukesbiri on Sunday last [the 16th], and offered to do him homage; but, as the K. had not his council with him, he prorogued the day for doing homage to London, declaring that such prorogation should not redound to the said K. or his heirs' prejudice." The annals of Waverly state that the homage was rendered in a great parliament at Westminster, in the middle of the month of October, but say nothing as to its nature. According to the Scottish account presented in the Register of Dunfermlyn, and followed by Mr. Robertson, Alexander became Edward's liegeman "for all the lands I hold of you in England, saving my own kingdom." The bishop of Norwich added: "And reserving to the king of England the right which he has to homage for your kingdom." Alexander replied in a loud voice: "To homage for my kingdom of Scotland none has right save God alone, and of God only do I hold my kingdom." After Bruce had sworn fealty, Alexander again added: "For the lands I hold of you in England." This account is substantiated by a papal bull of June 27, 1299. The Scottish church was independent of English control, being directly subject to the see of Rome, like the English church. After the competitors for the Scottish crown had submitted themselves to Edward's overlordship, his interference with ecclesiastical affairs in the north called forth a spirited remonstrance from Boniface VIII, in which he cites a number of precedents, showing that Edward had gone beyond his rights, not only in the ecclesiastical, but in the temporal affairs of Scotland. After showing that the kings of England had repeatedly guaranteed the liberty and independence of the kingdom of Scotland, he continues:

> Et cum etiam Rex ipse pro Tyndaliae, ac de Peynerrae terris, in Regno Angliae positis, se ad tuam praesentiam personaliter contulisset, tibi fidelitatem solitam impensurus; idem in praestatione fidelitatis hujusmodi, multis tunc praesentibus, vivae vocis oraculo publice declaravit, quod pro terris eisdem sitis tantum in Anglia, non ut Rex Scotiae, neque pro Scotiae Regno fidelitatem exhibebat eandem; quinimmo palam extitit protestatus, quod pro Regno ipso tibi fidelitatem praestare, seu facere aliquatenus non debebat, ut pote tibi penitus non subjecto, tuque sic oblatam fidelitatem hujusmodi admisisti.

It was the last homage rendered by Scottish kings in the direct line of MacAlpin.[1]

The pleasantest of relations between the kingdoms continued during the reign of Alexander. Favors are cheerfully granted to the young prince and princess of Scotland by their uncle, Edward, and any violation of Alexander's rights or liberties receive speedy justice.[2] In 1281 the princess Margaret, now in her twenty-first year, was married to Eric, king of Norway. The next year her brother married the daughter of Guy, count of Flanders. Within a year both prince and princess were in their graves — the latter leaving

The Failure of the Royal Line in Scotland

---

[1] Bain, Cal. Docts., II, Introd., p. xi, Nos. 63, 93, 104, 107, 109, 112-16, 119-23, 125-6, 128; Foedera, II, pp. 109, 136, 824; Triveti, Annales, p. 299; Early Kings, II, pp. 112, 424.

[2] In 1284 Edward requested from the pope, Martin IV, a grant of the tenths in Scotland for the relief of the Holy Land. It was granted only in case the king of Scotland consented, and on condition that Edward should personally assume the cross, and out of the money levied supply the wants of the Scotch crusaders. (Foedera, I, p. 274.)

an only child, Margaret, "the maiden of Norway." The prince had been the idol of the nation, the joy of his father's heart. His dying words — " Before tomorrow's sunrise the sun of Scotland will have set "— were echoed in " the boundless grief of the whole people, the tears and groans of all the clergy, and the endless sobs of the king and the magnates." A letter to Edward from the widowed and childless king — the only son of an only son — a letter full of the pathos of a great sorrow, is still preserved among the English archives. In it Alexander thanks him for his sympathy, and reminds him

. . . . that, though death has carried off all of his blood in Scotland, one yet remains, the child of his own dearest daughter, the K.'s niece, the late queen of Norway, now under divine providence the heir apparent of Scotland. Much good may yet be in store for them, and death only can dissolve their league of amity.

Measures were at once taken by the bereaved king to secure the succession, and in a parliament at Scone, Margaret, the princess of Norway, was acknowledged by the nobles as their sovereign, failing any heirs who might yet be born to the king or to the wife of the deceased prince; her dominions included the isles, Man, Tyndale, and Penrith, in addition to the kingdom of Scotland. The death of both Alexander's children led to his marriage with Joleta, daughter of the count of Dreux, in 1285. But the fate of Scotland and the last male of her kingly line was at hand. The air was full of forebodings, and the darkest fears of loyal Scotsmen were realized when the news came that the king, attempting to go from Edinburgh castle to Kinghorn in the early gloom of a wild March night, had been thrown by a stumbling horse, and found by his attendants at the foot of the cliffs, dead. The Lowland poet voiced the cry of many a heart in Scotland when he wrote:

> Chryst borne into Virgynyté
> Succour Scotland, and remede,
> That stad is in perplexyté.[1]

[1] Bain, Cal. Docts., II, Nos. 155-60, 197, 220-1, 224, 241, 247, 248, 250, 273; Early Kings, II, pp. 114, 117; Fordun, An., §§ 63, 64; Foedera, II, p. 274.

The two Alexanders were long remembered as the kings of peace. During their reigns the bonds uniting them with England were constantly drawn closer. Yet it was the alliance of younger and elder brothers, rather than of lord and vassal. There will be few to dispute the judgment which Lord Hailes has passed on Alexander III, and which, says Mr. Bain, the documents of the period fully bear out: "His conduct toward the neighboring kingdom was uniformly candid and wise. He maintained that amity with England which interest as well as relation to its sovereigns required; yet he never submitted to any concession which might injure the independency of the kingdom and church of Scotland."[1]

The heir to the throne was a child of tender years, residing in Norway. By common consent a regency was appointed in Scotland, consisting of six members. But letters had already been forwarded to Edward from the grave of the dead sovereign, by the bishops of St. Andrews and Glasgow, and the magnates, asking his counsel and advice. He was nearest of kin to the lonely child. Alexander had specially commended her to his protection, plainly intimating that through her might come about a natural union between the two kingdoms. It would have been strange indeed if Edward—though honestly seeking to deal fairly with the little maid of Norway and the kingdom of his late brother-in-law—had been blind to the political opportunity which lay before him. The Scots also seem to have regarded a union with England as the best resource open to them. Both parties, therefore, sought to bring about the marriage of the princess Margaret with the crown prince of England. Honorius IV sanctioned the marriage on the ground that the king could find no equal alliances for his children save within the forbidden degrees. It was also urged that if Margaret married any other prince, war would arise between Scotland and England, and Edward be prevented from going on his promised crusade. Representatives appointed October 3, 1289, by the guardians of the

[1] Annals, Vol. I, p. 202.

realm of Scotland, met with others from England and Norway, at Salisbury—"salvis tamen, in omnibus et singulis, et per omnia libertate et honore Regni Scotiae." They were to negotiate a treaty for the conveyance of Margaret from Norway, either to Scotland, or to the care of her uncle, Edward. But there is no doubt both parties had in mind the subsequent marriage treaty concluded at Brigham, on the north bank of the Tweed (July 18, 1290). The chief. articles, proposed by the English to the "nobiles viros, Comites, et Barones, totamque Communitatem Regni Scotiae," and accepted in their behalf by the guardians of the realm of Scotland, were:

1. That the rights, laws, liberties, and customs of Scotland should remain forever entire and inviolable, throughout the whole realm and its marches, *saving always the right of the king of England, and of all others which, before the date of this treaty, belonged to him, or any of them, in the marches, or elsewhere, or which ought to belong to him, or any of them, in all time coming.*

This, says Lord Hailes, was "*the fatal salvo*, so artfully devised as to bear the semblance of impartiality, and to prevent all suspicion of sinister views. Yet in it the foundations were laid for England's claim of feudal sovereignity over Scotland."

2. Failing Margaret and Edward, or either of them, without issue, the kingdom shall return to the nearest heirs, to whom it ought of right to return, wholly, freely, absolutely, and without any subjection; so that hereby nothing shall either *accrue or decrease* to the king of England, to his heirs, or to any one else.

The kingdom of Scotland shall remain separate and divided from England, free in itself, and without subjection, according to the right boundaries and marches, as heretofore. (Salvo as in Art. I.)

4. No native of Scotland shall, in any case, whether of covenant made, or crime committed in Scotland, be compelled to answer out of the kingdom, contrary to the laws and usages of Scotland, heretofore of reason observed.

A final protestation was added to the treaty: "That the premises shall be so understood, as that nothing may thereby accrue to, or decrease from, the right of either kingdom, or of the sovereigns thereof." The intent and purpose of this document are perfectly clear. Had the child-queen lived, the liberties of Scotland, so jealously watched over, might have survived unharmed. These provisions were ratified by Edward at Northampton, August 28, 1290.[1]

Great preparations were made for bringing this "child of so many hopes" to her kingdom and future home. But suddenly, in the midst of them all, the prospect of a peaceful alliance was overclouded by the rumor of the maiden's death at Orkney, while en route to her realm. Trouble and despair settled on the unhappy land of the north. The bishop of St. Andrews wrote to the king of England, urging him to come to the march without delay, to prevent bloodshed. No provision had been made for the succession in case of Margaret's death. That possibility must have been foreseen, and it seems as if the nobles had purposely left it unprovided for, in order to further their own selfish ends. Indeed, a bond had been entered into between Robert Bruce and other nobles, as early as September, 1286, for mutual defense and assistance, which looked to the establishment of Bruce as king, "according to the ancient custom hitherto approved and observed in the kingdom of Scotland." He was but one of many who, through the failure of direct heirs to the crown, waited for some turn of fate which might open to them the path to royal honors. Thus it was that Scotland—torn by rival factions and left to the mercy of a king, who, great as he was, and just as he wished to be considered, could not resist the temptation to extend his power beyond the limits of right and justice—for the second time in her history passed under the hand of an English overlord. But this was chiefly brought about by the southern barons, many of them of Norman descent, holding lands in England, and sympathizing with their English overlord. The Scottish Commons, not yet risen to marked power, steadily resisted any such concessions, and preserved untainted that loyalty and devotion to the national cause which found a

[1] Foedera, II, pp. 431, 450, 482; Hailes' Annals, I, p. 208; Stevenson, Docts., I, pp. 105, 111, 162; Bain, II, Nos. 298, 392; Fordun, An., § 68.

leader in the noble Bruce, and saw the dawn of a new day of independence in the victory of Bannockburn.[1]

NOTE (*cf.* p. 139).—During the reign of Henry III, the *Inspeximus* charter had its rise. It was nothing more than the royal acknowledgment of having seen and confirmed some diploma granted by the king, or his predecessors, without altering the nature of the original grant. On attaining his majority, Henry announced that no charters, either lay or ecclesiastical, would be regarded as of moment till they had been renewed under the king's new seal.[2] Among the charters thus confirmed is one which bears on the question of Lothian. It is an *Inspeximus* by Henry of a charter by King John, to the prior and monks of Durham, of all the lands, tithes, churches, and tenures, belonging to the Priory — some of which are found north of the Tweed. It is not strange that the monks of Durham, holding lands on the borders, where they would suffer most from the ravages of war, should seek confirmation of their charters at the hands of both kings, irrespective of the location of the holdings. Frequent instances occur.[3] The question at issue is, Did John, in this charter make new grants to Durham, north of the Tweed, thereby evidencing his superiority over that region; or, did he merely confirm grants already made by the kings of England and Scotland? Mr. Bain says this charter "is interesting and valuable, as distinctly showing the superiority of the English kings over that district" [Lothian]. It begins: "Sciatis nos concessisse et *confirmasse* in puram et perpetuam elemosinam, Domino et Sancto Cuthberto," . . . .[4] There follows a long list of lands in England, and then: "The church of Norham, with its chapels, lands, and waters; and the vill of Schoreswirth (Surwirth), beyond the river of Tweed; Coldingham, with its church and pertinents, viz., Haldecambehus, with the church, Lummesdenes, Reynton, and Grenewude, and the two Rystones, Aldegrave, Swynewde, and the two Eystones, with the mills and port, and Prendregeste, with the mill; Ederham and its church, with all its chapels; and the two Swintones, with the

[1] Bain, Cal. Docts., II, No. 464; Nat. MSS. Scot., I, No. LXX; Stevenson, Docts., I, p. 22.

[2] Rotuli Chart., Introd., pp. iv ff.

[3] Bain, Cal. Docts., I, Nos. 2216, 2231, 2275-6.

[4] St. Cuthbert's was originally located at Lindesfarne, and its lands extended as far north as the Forth. It was removed to Durham in 995.

church; the church of Berewick, with its pertinents; Fyswik, with the church; Paxtone; Nessebyte, with the mill; the church of Edinham, with the chapel of Stichehulle, and its pertinents; and, moreover, all that they possess in Lothian (Lodoneyo), by will (voluntate) of the monks of St. Cuthbert, to be disposed of as the charter of Edgar K. of Scots attests. Besides these, all that the kings of England or Scotland, or the bishops of Durham, have given or granted to them, in perpetual alms."[1] The basis for this charter was laid in the days of William Rufus. Under Malcolm III, two parties had developed in Scotland, one purely Scottish in spirit, the other sympathizing with the English alliance, made up chiefly of the foreigners who came in with Queen Margaret, and of the Normans and Saxons dwelling in the Lowlands. On the death of Malcolm, the Scottish party placed his brother Donald Bain on the throne. Malcolm's son by Ingebiorg, Duncan, a hostage at the English court, had continued to reside there after his release. With the consent of William Rufus he now succeeded in driving Donald from the throne of Scotland, but was in turn surprised, his followers killed, and he himself allowed to rule only on condition of renouncing his alliance with the detested *Saxons*. He was killed soon after and Donald was restored. Malcolm had left three sons by Queen Margaret. With the consent of William, but mainly through the efforts of Margaret's brother, Edgar Aetheling, Donald was again driven from his throne, and Edgar, the eldest son of Malcolm and Margaret, was established as king of Scotland. In the group of charters which follows, the first is by Duncan, granting Tiningham and other lands to St. Cuthbert. The expression "constans hereditarie Rex Scotiae" is thought to throw doubt on the authenticity of the charter. It certainly expresses the only principle on which the Scots consented to permit him to rule over them.[2] (1) The first of Edgar's charters (1097–1107), relating to lands north of the Tweed, is one in which he styles himself "by the grace of God, King of the Scots," and grants to St. Cuthbert's "Fiswic tam in terris quam in aquis et cum omnibus sibi adiacentibus; et nominatim illam terram que iacet inter Horuerdene et Cnapedene . . . . liberam et quietam

[1] Bain, I, Introd., p. lxiii, No. 1924; Rotuli Chart., I, p. 119.

[2] Nat. MSS. Scot., I, Introd., p. viii, p. 4; *cf.* Raine, North Durham, pp. 374–6. "The lands granted were part of the endowment of the see of St. Andrew's, to which they again reverted, probably when Duncan's usurpation of the Scottish throne came to an end." (Had. and Stubbs, Counc., Vol. II, Pt. I, p. 165, note.)

tenendam et habendam, et ad uoluntatem monachorum Sancti Cuthberti domini mei disponendam." Edgar was present at the dedication of the church of St. Mary at Coldingham, and (2) granted in endowment (1097–8) "the whole town of Swintun, with its marches as Liulf held it," under the same tenure as above. Another charter (3) includes Paxton to be held on the same conditions. The grant of Coldingham to Durham includes the messuages of Aldcambus, Lummesdene, Regnintun, Ristun, Swinewde, Farndun, Eitun, "The other Eitun," Prenegest, Cramesmuthe. These also are to be freely disposed of at the will of the monks of Durham forever. (4) The original of the next charter granted by Edgar has been lost, but "good and unsuspected copies"[1] have been preserved. This is the well known charter in which are the words "Edgarus filius Malcolmi Regis Scottorum *totam terram de Lodoneio et regnum Scotie dono domini mei Willelmi Anglorum Regis et paterna hereditate possidens, consilio praedicti domini Regis W. et fidelium meorum.* . . ." Accompanying this is a charter of William Rufus, in which he confirms the grant of Edgar to Durham. It begins "Sciatis me concessisse Deo . . . . terras in Lodoneio quas Edgarus rex filius Malcolmi regis Scottorum . . . . *me concedente* donauit," and includes the messuage of Berwick, with those of Greidene, Leinhale, Dylsterhale, Brycgham, Ederham, Cirnside, Hyltun, Blacedre, Cynebrihtham, Hotun, Reinintun, Paxtun, Fugeldene, Morthintun, Lambertun, "the other Lambertun," Haedrintun, Fiscwic, Horeford, Upsetinton. Also the messuage of Coldingham with those of Aldcambus, Lummesdene, Ristun, Suinestun, Farndun, Eitun, "the other Eitun," Prenegest, Crammesmuthe, Haedentun. Another charter (5) contains the words "Edgarus Dei gratia Rex Scottorum. . . . Sciatis nos *ex licentia Willelmi Regis Anglie superioris domini regni Scotiae* . . . ." Even Palgrave admits it to be a forgery, possibly by Hardynge. Raine considers (4) to be genuine and is supported by Cosmo Innes and Bain. They point out the distinction which Edgar made between his title to Lothian, which he held by gift (*donum*) of the English king, and to the kingdom of Scotland, which he held independently as his *paterna hereditas*.[2] Innes represents the consensus of expert authority on this question when he says: "It is now held, without much differ-

[1] Cosmo Innes, Nat. MSS. Scot., Introd., I, p. viii.

[2] Haddan regards both (4) and (5) as forgeries, and says Raine's arguments "fail to establish any distinction in favor of (4)." (H. and S., Counc., II, Pt. I, p. 166, note.)

ence of opinion, that Edgar may have wished to acknowledge, or was not minded to dispute, some claim of property or superiority of William in these Berwickshire lands, and that the monks of Durham were well pleased to hold them by the grants of both kings. Neither party dreamt of giving or taking a right of superiority to the king of England over the kingdom of Scotland. Sir Francis Palgrave, in his Anglo-Saxon zeal, had worked himself up to be of a different opinion; but *pace tanti viri*, the question has been settled by more temperate historians; and an Englishman who knew more of the evidence than any man of his time has wound up his argument thus: 'That homage was paid from time to time is certain, but it was for territories held of the English crown and not for Scotland at large' (Raine's History of North Durham, p. 377)."[1]

These charters of Edgar, issued in the spirit of his English mother Margaret, were duly confirmed by his brothers, Alexander as king, and David as earl, though as king David simply grants the lands in Lothian, "to wit, Coldingham, Aldecambus, Lumesdene, Prenegest, Eitun, the other Eitun, and Crammesmuth, Lambertun and the other Lambertun, Paxtun, Fiswic, and Swinton."[2] No mention is made of the other lands granted by Edgar and confirmed by William Rufus.

The question does not reappear till the reign of John. He confirms to the church of Durham all the lands, etc., including those granted by Edgar. Here is an *appearance* of English superiority north of the Tweed which the sources elsewhere forbid us to entertain as a permanent fact. An explanation of this contradiction may be found (1) in the fact that these lands were "to be freely disposed of at the will of the monks of Durham forever;" or (2) in some of the secret agreements between John and William the Lion. But the simplest and most natural explanation of the charter is found in the bonds which were knitting north and south into one great family. Under these conditions the exact line of demarcation between the two sovereignties, and perfect equity in the exercise of kingly powers, might be found wanting, without thereby implying any permanent change of conditions. It is tolerably certain that William Rufus exercised some sort of superiority in Lothian during the reign of Edgar. There is no evidence that that superiority continued after David reunited the sover-

---

[1] Nat. MSS. Scot., I, pp. 5, 6; Introd., p. ix; Bain, I, Introd., p. lxiii; Palgrave, Scot. Docts., I, p. ccxvi.

[2] Nat. MSS. Scot., I, pp. 7-8.

eignty of Scotland, north and south of the Forth, in his own person. Palgrave's assertion that the king of Scots had the same jurisdiction in Lothian as in Tynedale, and held it by the same allegiance, is not sustained by the sources. This fact makes it necessary to explain John's charter in some other way than on the ground of superiority over Lothian. Even granting that Lothian was held on as free conditions as a *Palatine* county of England, it should have reverted to the escheator on the death of its holder. Tynedale as a regality does so in every instance, Lothian never. Tynedale is included in the compotus of lands in England of which Alexander III received seizin; Lothian is not. When Balliol swore fealty and rendered homage, late in 1292, to Edward, "King of England and Superior Lord of the Kingdom of Scotland," he received possession of his kingdom, and in January, 1293, had seizin of the Isle of Man without further homage. Nearly a year elapsed before he regained his English fiefs. Lothian was not among them, nor is it once mentioned. Two inquisitions (under writs dated at Newcastle-on-Tyne, January 1, 1292) at Carlisle and at Werk in Tynedale, made by English jurors before the escheator *citra* Trent, "find that the late Alexander K. of Scots held *in capite* of the K. of England the manors of Penrith, Soureby, Langwathby, Salkild, Karlatton, Scotteby, delivering a year old goshawk annually at the castle of Carlisle, ... and doing homage to the Kings of England. They are worth 200l. yearly. John de Balliol is the next heir and is 30 years of age." The same finding is made regarding Tynedale, except that the lands are held by the sole service of homage and are worth 108l. yearly.[1] The king commanded the escheator to put Balliol in possession, provided that before or in the quinzaine of St. Michael next he does homage. A distinct line was thus drawn between homage for his kingdom and for his English lands. In October, 1293, he renders homage, as his predecessors, the kings of Scotland, had done, not for his kingdom, which included Lothian and the Isle of Man, but "*de omnibus terris et tenementis*" which he holds "*in capite in Anglia*," viz., Tynedale, the above mentioned lands in Cumberland, and his purparty of the honor of Huntingdon.[2] Had Lothian been aught but an integral portion of the kingdom of Scotland, it must have appeared in the record of these transactions. Henry's Inspeximus charter, therefore,

[1] The annual entry in the Rolls for Tynedale — held by Scottish kings from Henry II to Edward I — is 10l.

[2] Bain, II, Nos. 664-5, 669, 679; Foedera, II, p. 616.

was simply a confirmation of John's confirmation of Edgar's charter, which had been first confirmed by William Rufus. If English superiority over Lothian ever existed, it was of a temporary and exceptional character, and did not form a part of the continuous feudal relations between the kings of England and Scotland.

BIBLIOGRAPHY.

SOURCES.

SCOTCH RECORD PUBLICATIONS.

Calendar of Documents relating to Scotland, preserved in her Majesty's Public Record Office, London. Ed., Joseph Bain. Edinburgh.

SCHEDULE OF RECORDS EXAMINED, VOL. I (1881).

EXCHEQUER.

	No. of Rolls
Pipe Rolls, 31 Henry I to 56 Henry III,	116
Chancellor's Rolls, 2 Henry II to Henry III (65),	9
Originalia Rolls, 11 Henry II,	33
Memoranda Rolls, 9 Richard I to 1 John,	1
Memoranda Rolls, 10 John,	1
Memoranda Rolls (Q. R.), 1 to 57 Henry III,	45
Memoranda Rolls (L. T. R.), 1 to 56 Henry III,	48
Wardrobe Accounts, 36–57 Henry III,	35
"The Red Book" of Exchequer,	
Liber "A," Chapter House,	
Issue Rolls (Pells), 25–47 Henry III,	12
Misae Roll, 14 John,	1

CHANCERY.

Patent Rolls, 3 John to 57 Henry III,	90
Close Rolls, 6 John to 57 Henry III,	94
Charter Rolls, 1 John to 56 Henry III,	66
Oblata, 1–9 John,	4
Misae, 11 John,	1
Praestita, 7–12,	2
Fine Rolls, 6 John to 56 Henry III,	69
Liberate Rolls, 2 John to 57 Henry III,	47
French Rolls, 26 Henry III,	1
Chancery Files (*temp.* John and Henry III),	13 bundles
Inquisitions post mortem (*temp.* Henry III),	
Tower Miscellaneous Rolls, Scottish affairs, Portfolio No. 459,	
Papal Bulls, Innocent IV 97, } Papal Bulls, Alexander IV 28, }	125
Royal Letters,	
Miscellaneous Portfolios, Nos. 7, 9, 10, 15, 16, 41,	

QUEEN'S BENCH.

Coram Rege Rolls, 6 Richard I to 57 Henry III,	172
Assize Rolls, 40–53 Henry II,	8

COMMON PLEAS.

Feet of Fines, Richard I to Henry III,	81

DUCHY OF LANCASTER.

Charters,	3 vols
Grants (in boxes) Box ("A,")	

STATE PAPER OFFICE.

Privy seal,	3 bundles

VOL. II (1884).

EXCHEQUER.

	No. of Rolls, etc.
Pipe Rolls, 1–35 Edward I,	35
Chancellor's Rolls, 1–15 Edward I,	15
Originalia Rolls, 1–21,	19
Memoranda Rolls (Q. R.), 1–35 Edward I,	31
Memoranda Rolls (L. T. R.), 1–20,	17
Miscellanea (Q. R.), 1–35 Edward I.	—
Miscellanea (Q. R. Army), 1–35 Edward I,	—
Miscellanea (Q. R. Wardrobe), 1–35 Edward I,	—
Miscellanea Treasury of Receipt, 1–35 Edward I,	—
Liber "A," Chapter House,	
Paper Documents, Chapter House, 7 Portfolios,	*v. y.*
Scots Documents, Chapter House,	

CHANCERY.

Patent Rolls, 1–35 Edward I,	37
Close Rolls, 1–35 Edward I,	35
Charter Rolls, 2–35 Edward I,	34
Fine Rolls, 1–28 Edward I,	28
Liberate Rolls, 1–35 Edward I,	35
Chancery Files, 1–35 Edward I,	11 bundles
Inquisitions post mortem, 1–35 Edward I,	
Tower miscellaneous Rolls, Portfolio No. 459,	
Papal Bulls (Alexander IV–Clement V),	170
Royal Letters,	
Miscellaneous Portfolios, Nos. 11, 41, 475,	
Parliamentary Petitions,	
Writs of Privy Seal (Tower),	17 bundles

QUEEN'S BENCH.

Assize Rolls, Northumberland, Cumberland, Westmoreland, etc.,

DUCHY OF LANCASTER.

Charters, ... 3 vols.
Grants (in boxes) "A," "B," etc., ...

Documents Illustrative of the History of Scotland from the death of Alexander III to the accession of Robert Bruce. Ed. Joseph Stevenson. 2 vols. 1870.
Facsimiles of the National MSS. of Scotland. Introd., Cosmo Innes. 3 vols.

PUBLICATIONS OF THE RECORD COMMISSIONERS.

Rotuli Chartarum, in Turri Londinensi Asservati. Ed., Thomas Duffus Hardy. Vol. I. 1837.
Documents and Records illustrating the History of Scotland, and Transactions between England and Scotland; preserved in the treasury of her Majesty's Exchequer. Ed. Francis Palgrave. Vol. I. 1837.
Ancient Laws and Institutes of England. Ed., Benjamin Thorpe. 2 vols. 1840.

SURTEES SOCIETY.

Historiae Dunelmensis Scriptores Tres. Ed., James Raine. London, 1839.

ENGLISH HISTORICAL SOCIETY.

Codex Diplomaticus, Aevi Saxonici. Ed., Johannis M. Kemble. 6 vols. 1839.
Bedae Historia Ecclesiastica Gentis Anglorum. Ed., Josephus Stevenson. 1838.
Florentii Wigorniensis Chronicon ex Chronicis. Ed., Benjamin Thorpe. 2 vols. 1848.
Historia Rerum Anglicarum Willelmi de Newburgh. Ed., Hans Claude Hamilton. 1856.
Chronicon Walteri de Hemingburgh. Ed., Hans Claude Hamilton. 2 vols. 1848.
F. Nicholai Triveti Annales. Ed., Thomas Hog. 1845.

CHRONICLES AND MEMORIALS (ROLLS SERIES).

Descriptive Catalogue of Manuscripts relating to the History of Great Britain and Ireland. Ed., Thomas Duffus Hardy. 3 vols. 1862-1871.
Anglo-Saxon Chronicle. Ed. and Trans., Benjamin Thorpe. 2 vols. 1861.
Gesta Regis Henrici Secundi Benedicti Abbatis. Ed., William Stubbs. 2 vols. 1867.
Chronica Magistri Rogeri de Hovedene. Ed., William Stubbs. 4 vols. 1868-1871.
Memoriale Fratris Walteri de Coventria. Ed., William Stubbs. 2 vols. 1872-1873.
Radulfi de Diceto Opera Historica. Ed., William Stubbs. 2 vols. 1876.
Willelmi Monachi Malmesbiriensis de Regum Gestis Anglorum. Ed., William Stubbs. 2 vols. 1887-1889.
Henrici Archidiaconi Huntenduniensis Historia Anglorum. Ed., Thomas Arnold. 1879.
Historical Works of Symeon of Durham. Ed., Thomas Arnold. 2 vols. 1882-1885.
Eadmeri Historia Novorum in Anglia. Ed., Martin Rule. 1884.
Chronicles of the Reigns of Stephen, Henry II, and Richard I. Ed., Richard Howlett. Vols. III and IV. 1884-1890.
Chronica Rogeri de Wendover. Ed., Henry Gay Hewlett. 3 vols. 1886-1889.

Matthaei Parisiensis, Chronica Majora. Ed., Henry Richards Luard. 7 vols. 1872–1884.

——— Historia Anglorum. Ed., Frederic Madden. 3 vols. 1866–1869.

War of the Gaedhil with the Gaill. Ed., James Henthorn Todd. 1867.

Ricardi de Cirencestria Speculum Historiale. Ed., John E. B. Mayor. 1863–1869.

Brut y Twysogion. Ed., John Williams ab Ithel. 1860.

Works of Giraldus Cambrensis. Ed., J. S. Brewer, James F. Dimock, and George F. Warner. 8 vols. 1861–1891.

Capgrave's Chronicle of England. Ed., Francis Charles Hingeston. 1858.

Annales Monastici. Ed., Henry Richards Luard. Vols. I–III. 1864–1866.

HISTORIANS OF SCOTLAND.

Johannis de Fordun Chronica Gentis Scotorum. Ed., William Forbes Skene. 1871.

Androw, of Wyntoun. Orygynale Cronykil of Scotland. Ed., David Laing. 3 vols. 1871.

MISCELLANEOUS.

Foedera, Conventiones, Litterae, etc. Thoma Rymer. 2d Ed., Vols. I and II. London, 1727.

Syllabus in English of Rymer's Foedera. Ed., Thomas Duffus Hardy. 3 vols. 1869–1885.

Liber Niger Scaccarii. Thomas Hearnii. 2 vols. London, 1774.

General Introduction to Domesday Book. Henry Ellis. 2 vols. 1833.

Councils and Ecclesiastical Documents relating to Great Britain and Ireland. Ed., after Spelman and Wilkins, by Haddan and Stubbs. 3 vols. Oxford, 1869.

Select Charters. Ed., William Stubbs. 7th Ed. Oxford., 1890.

Historiae Anglicanae Scriptores X. Ed., Roger Twysden. London, 1652.

Ecclesiastical History of England and Normandy. Ordericus Vitalis. (Bohn Library.)

Flowers of History. Matthew of Westminster. (Bohn Library.)

Annals of the Caledonians, Picts and Scots. Ed., Joseph Ritson. 2 vols. Edinburgh, 1828.

AUTHORITIES.

Bacon, Francis: Life and Letters of. Ed., James Spedding. 7 vols. London, 1890.

Burton, John Hill: History of Scotland. 2d Ed., 8 vols. Edinburgh and London.

Eyton, Robert William: Court, Household, and Itinerary of Henry II. London, 1878.

Freeman, Edward A.: History of the Norman Conquest in England. Vols. I and II, 3d Ed.; III and IV, 2d Ed.; V, 1st Ed. Oxford, 1877.

——— Reign of William Rufus and the Accession of Henry I. 2 vols. Oxford, 1882.

Gardiner, Samuel R.: Student's History of England. New York, 1895.

Green, John Richard: Conquest of England. New York.

——— History of the English People. 4 vols. New York.

Guest, Edwin: Origines Celticae. 2 vols. London, 1883.

Hailes, (Dalyrimple, David): Annals of Scotland. 3 vols. Edinburgh, 1797.

Hume, David: History of England. 6 vols. New York, 1879.

Innes, Thomas: Critical Essay on the Ancient Inhabitants of the Northern Parts of Britain or Scotland. (Historians of Scotland Series.)
Lingard, John: History of England. 5th Ed. 10 vol. London, 1849.
Lyttelton, George Lord: History of the Life of King Henry the Second and of the Age in which he lived. 6 vols. London, 1769.
Madox, Thomas: History and Antiquities of the Exchequer of the Kings of England. 2 vols. London, 1769.
Makower, Felix: Constitutional History and Constitution of the Church of England. English translation. London, 1895.
Norgate, Kate: England under the Angevin Kings. 2 vols. London, 1887.
Palgrave, Francis: History of Normandy and of England. 4 vols. London, 1878.
———— Rise and Progress of the English Commonwealth. 2 vols. London, 1832.
Pinkerton, John: Enquiry into the History of Scotland. 2 vols. 1814.
Ridpath, George: Border History of England and Scotland. Berwick, 1848.
Robertson, Edward William: History of Scotland under her Early Kings. 2 vols. Edinburgh, 1862.
Robertson, William: History of Scotland. 15th Ed. 3 vols. London, 1797.
Round, John Horace: Feudal England. London, 1895.
Skene, William Forbes: Celtic Scotland. 3 vols. Edinburgh, 1876.
Wakeman, Henry Offley, and Arthur Hassall, Eds.: Essays introductory to the Study of the English Constitution. London, 1891.

SPECIAL ARTICLES.

Tennyson, Hallam: Translation of the Ode on Brunanburh. Contemporary Review, November, 1879.
Freeman, Edward A.: Historical Essays. First Series. 4th Ed. London, 1886.

www.ingramcontent.com/pod-product-compliance
Lightning Source LLC
Chambersburg PA
CBHW032158160426
43197CB00008B/976